British Railway Disasters

British Railway Disasters

Lessons learned from tragedies on the tracks

Robin Jones

To my big brother Stewart – my
greatest railway friend

First published as Britain's Railway Disasters in 2016
By Mortons Media Group Ltd.

This edition published in 2019 by Gresley Books,
an imprint of Mortons Books Ltd.
Media Centre
Morton Way
Horncastle LN9 6JR
www.mortonsbooks.co.uk

ISBN 978-1-911658-01-6

Typeset by ATG Media
Printed and bound by Gutenberg Press, Malta.

10 9 8 7 6 5 4 3 2 1

Contents

INTRODUCTION

Britain gave the world the greatest transport invention since the wheel. In 1802, Cornish mining engineer Richard Trevithick ran his first steam railway locomotive at Ironbridge. Two years later, on the Pen-y-darren Tramroad near Merthyr Tydfil, he gave his first public demonstration of one. It would be a somewhat erroneous cliché to say the world from then on never looked back, because it took nearly a decade before his invention was taken seriously. Horses were state-of-the-art transport, and Trevithick's inventions – he also built road steam engines – were at first considered very much in the novelty category. A shortage of horses, brought about because of the military requirements for vast numbers to be used in the Napoleonic Wars, led to mine owners in the north of England looking anew at Trevithick's ideas, and several mining engineers built their own primitive railway engines, with varying degrees of success.

However, it was only with the opening of the Liverpool & Manchester Railway that the Rubicon was crossed, and steam locomotives, as opposed to equines, cable haulage or manpower, became the premium transport mode. Within 20 years, Britain found itself criss-crossed by a network of trunk railways, linking city to city and replacing journeys that once took days by stagecoach and even longer by canal barge with trips that lasted a few hours. The watching world eagerly took up this new transport technology. Railways were a great liberating force, allowing people to move from one part of the country to another, taking employment in areas away from their traditional homes, while allowing the bulk transport of raw materials and finished products to boost industry like never before. Greater mobility led to better social conditions, and in turn the railways were joined by motor road transport and aircraft; the invention of which followed in their wake. There has, however, always been one core problem, one big drawback, with one of man's greatest inventions… and that is man.

Railways were designed by people for people, and run by people, with all of their human failings. That meant that while they brought about untold benefits, they've always had a fallible human downside. Trevithick's brilliant concept, which was devised with the aim of hauling heavy beam engine components from the nearest port to tin and copper mines, was honed to perfection by father and son George and Robert Stephenson in *Rocket*, which established the pattern for future steam locomotive evolution. Yet if any of today's health and safety inspectors were asked to look over early steam locomotives, they would undoubtedly have been horrified. They would have been condemned as disasters waiting to happen on wheels; the high incidence of boiler explosions in the 19th century was testament to that fact. With hindsight, it appears that contemporary audiences dazzled by the novelty of a self-propelled machine never stopped to consider basic safety matters, or the consequences if anything went wrong.

The world's first widely reported railway tragedy was the death of MP William Huskisson on the opening day of the Liverpool & Manchester Railway, crushed by *Rocket* – which had no brakes. It took another three years before a minor accident on a crossing at Bagworth, in Leicestershire, it has been claimed, led to the addition of warning whistles on locomotives. From Trevithick's day, railways have been on a learning curve. Much of the evolution of railways has taken place only in response to accidents and disasters, by which very hard lessons are learned, or regrettably, in certain cases ignored. Dotted around the country are memorials to those who have died in railway accidents through no fault of their own, and the grief of the bereaved is never laid to rest. It comes as scant consolation to those who have lost family and friends, but out of darkness and despair a fresh beacon of light, one illuminating the way to a safer transport system, has often emerged.

Today, Britain's railways are among the safest in the world, but in their formative years it was a very different story. As our railway network mushroomed in the mid-1840s, it was unregulated, uncoordinated and, certainly by today's standards, highly dangerous – exploding boilers, broken rails, absence of signals, inadequate brakes, wooden carriages likely to catch fire from gas lighting and so on. In 2015, the Railway Inspectorate celebrated its 175th anniversary. To mark the occasion, on November 19 at Euston, Direct Rail Services' Class 57 No. 57306 was named *Her Majesty's Railway Inspectorate*. Founded in 1840, in the days of steam engines with huge shiny copper domes and no cab protection from the elements for the footplate crews, the body – now part of the Office of Rail and Road (known as the Office of Rail Regulation until recently, and referred to as such in many of the chapters) – carries on its excellent work in an era when the UK is planning a network of high-speed rail lines to further reduce travelling times between major cities. With the passing of the 1840 Railway Regulation Act, the Board of Trade appointed the first Railway Inspector to inspect construction and equipment of new railways, with safety concerns a top priority. That year, companies were required to give one month's notice of intention to open new railways. Two years later, inspectors were given the power to postpone the opening of new railways on safety grounds.

The year 1871 is held as a pivotal point in the history of railway safety, for it was then that the Regulation of Railways Act became law. The Act is regarded as the founding legislation of the modern inspectorate. It reinforced and consolidated previous provisions regarding the appointment of inspectors and the inspection of works. It gave the inspectors the formal powers to investigate railway accidents… and to recommend ways of avoiding them – a major turning point. The Railway Inspectorate's remit was widened in 1900 when it was given powers to investigate accidents to railway staff. Huge changes have been brought about since 1840 by the investigation, analysis, highlighting of problems and the making of recommendations on safety issues. It is impossible to quantify how many lives have been saved by the actions of this statutory body, and how it has helped accelerate the progress of safe and fast rail transport.

Continuous brakes, block signalling, cabs offering greater protection to drivers, rules for emergency evacuation from trains and guidance on boilers to avoid explosions all took safer railways forward. In recent decades, incidents of passengers being struck by trains while leaning out of windows or falling out of trains have led to automatic locking doors and sealed windows in new stock, and the end to the slam-door carriages across the network. Continuous welded rails eradicated fishplates and joints and led to fewer derailments because of the state of the track.

In 1994, the Safety Case Regulations were introduced, whereby every railway operator (trains, stations and infrastructure controller) had to have a Safety Case passed. A Safety Case shows that an operator has the resources, capability and commitment to ensure that safety practices are followed at all times and the safety of passengers and railway staff are not placed at risk. This evolution of railways through safety legislation will never end, as long as trains run. However much the public is horrified by reports of railway accidents, they must, however, be looked at in context. In numerical terms they are but a miniscule fraction of the number of deaths each year on Britain's roads, but when one, two or three people die on a train, it makes national headlines, and is written indelibly in railway history. Fatal car accidents rarely if ever earn such publicity. Yet there can never be any room for complacency while people place their lives in the hands of both train operators and in turn the regulatory bodies.

This book looks in detail at many, though by no means all, of Britain's worst railway crashes, but with an emphasis on the lessons that were learned from each, lessons which would save lives in the future – triumph from tragedy. A head-on collision between two trains at Thorpe St Andrew in Norfolk in 1874, for instance, left 25 people dead, and horrified the county and the nation, with the typical graphic engravings of the day widely appearing in newspapers and magazines. Yet telecommunications genius Edward Tyer responded by inventing a tablet system that reduced the likelihood of the human failings by station staff on that day and ensured that no two trains could be on the same stretch of line at the same time. Frustratingly, not all lifesaving inventions were widely adopted.

Many of the accidents covered in this volume, particularly those caused by suspected driver error, led to recommendations by inspectors and coroners that forms of automatic warning alerts, by which a driver would be notified by an alarm if he passed a signal at red, for instance, should be introduced across the board. Indeed, the Great Western Railway once again led the way by introducing Automatic Train Control in 1906, a system that could be used at high speed and which sounded a confirmation in the cab when a signal was passed at clear. However, other companies were slow to respond if they did at all, choosing to avoid the installation expense and rely on the experience and expertise of drivers and firemen who "knew the road". It was only in 1956 that British Railways introduced the Automatic Warning System (AWS) to help drivers observe and obey signals. It was based on a system developed by Alfred Ernest Hudd in the 1930s. Britain's worst peacetime rail disaster, the Harrow & Wealdstone crash of 1952, accelerated the introduction of AWS, but it would be a quarter of a century before a third of the national network was fitted with it.

The application of warning systems was still being debated decades on from that; drivers passing signals at danger were responsible for the Southall crash in 1997 and the Ladbroke Grove collision two years later. In the latter case, had an automatic train protection system been fitted and working it would have applied brakes to prevent the train passing a red signal. The nationwide installation of Automatic Train Protection, British Rail's preferred system, was recommended after the Clapham Junction disaster of 1988, but later abandoned because the safety benefits were considered not great enough to justify the cost. As we will see, in the accidents occurring since Privatisation in 1994, criticism has often been levelled at rail infrastructure companies, often by the trade unions, for placing profits before safety.

In some cases, however, lessons are hard to learn. A glaring example was the Great Heck disaster of 2001, caused by a freak chain of events said to have a 67 billion-to-one chance of occurring, which the railway could have done little to prevent, yet still it did. And while hindsight is a marvellous thing, for me it still beggars belief that lineside speed restriction warning signs reminding drivers to slow down were not universally adopted until after the Sutton Coldfield crash of 1955. It seems that there will always be the risk of human error, and the worst possible consequences arising from it. Yet in pursuit of the minimisation of that risk the science of railway safety continues to move forward, learning from every aberration no matter how small, and today in Britain we can be assured that it remains the safest form of land transport by a long way.

Chapter 1

1830 LIVERPOOL & MANCHESTER: THE FIRST WIDELY-PUBLICISED TRAGEDY

It is a long-held tradition, undoubtedly promoted by ill-advised schoolteachers, that the first death on the railways was that of William Huskisson MP, who at the age of 60 was run over by Stephenson's *Rocket* on the opening day of the Liverpool & Manchester Railway in 1830. However, the earliest-known railway fatality came in 1650, when two boys in Whickham, County Durham, were run down by a waggon on a wooden coal tramway. The railway concept itself, if only in the crude form of wheeled objects being guided by grooves cut in stone blocks, dates back to ancient Greece. Primitive tramways, or waggonways, became common in the north-east of England at the dawn of the industrial revolution, with coal waggons being hauled by horses or pushed by men out of mines and to the nearest transhipment point. Back in those days, fatalities in industrial concerns were often regarded as par for the course, and with newspapers still a comparative scarcity, probably many if not most of them went unreported. Such accidents on private tramways are not generally listed by historians as railway accidents, and so it is likely that there would have been many more.

Fast forward to Philadelphia, also in County Durham, in 1815, when on July 31, an early experimental railway locomotive, Brunton's Mechanical Traveller, otherwise known as the Steam Horse, suffered a boiler explosion. This type of locomotive, which was not adopted in general usage, ran on four wheels, but was pushed by mechanical feet, on a private industrial waggonway. The incident was the first railway accident causing major loss of life, as between 13 and 16 people, depending on which source you believe, were killed. It was also the first boiler explosion, a problem that would dog the early railways for decades. Brunton's locomotive was surrounded at the time by a crowd of curious sightseers, who formed the majority of the victims; although in most similar cases, only the footplate crew suffered. At the time, steam locomotive technology was still very much in its infancy. It was only 11 years since Cornishman Richard Trevithick had given his first public demonstration of a steam railway locomotive on the Pen-y-darren Tramroad near Merthyr Tydfil, and even though the concept had visibly proved itself, there was no rush of takers, most industrialists believing that it was just a novelty and that the future of motive power still lay with the horse. Consequently, when mine owners in the North-East began to show a greater interest in the steam locomotive, after horses were in short supply after military demands for them during the Napoleonic Wars, safety risks were by no means fully assessed.

In 1821, carpenter David Brook was walking home from Leeds along the private Middleton Railway in a sleet storm, when he was run over by a steam locomotive pulling a coal train. It was the first recorded case of someone being killed in a railway collision. In 1828, an unnamed woman – said to have been a blind beggar – from Eaglescliffe in County Durham was run over by a steam locomotive on the Stockton & Darlington Railway; the first recorded case of a female fatality on a railway. However, she has been overlooked by popular history. Clearly by no stretch of the imagination did this early victim have the public stature of a Member of Parliament, let alone one who was also president of the Board of Trade and treasurer of the Navy, and so her death would scarcely have warranted a mention in the national media of the day, if at all.

There were more to follow on what was the world's first public steam-operated railway. On March 19, 1828, the boiler of Stockton & Darlington Railway locomotive *Diligence* exploded at Simpasture Junction, where the line met the Clarence Railway at Newton Aycliffe. John Gillespie, a novice fireman, was taking his first journey aboard *Diligence*, driven by James Stephenson, elder brother of George Stephenson, 'father of the railways'. It was Gillespie's first day on the job, and he was under the watchful eye of the retiring fireman, Edward Corner, who was making his last journey. They stopped to pump fresh water into the tender. There was a strong wind blowing in the direction of the furnace, and this caused the fire to burn more brightly. Such early locomotives were often poor at maintaining steam pressure when they were in motion. However, when stationary and no longer using steam, the pressure built up, and the function of the safety valve was to vent the excess steam when it reached a certain pressure, usually about 50psi. However, some drivers routinely held the safety valve down when the engine was stationary, to build up an extra head of steam, though they were expressly banned from doing so by the company.

While there is no official record as to who was responsible, it must have been James Stephenson because he was the driver. Holding down *Diligence*'s safety valve would have been dangerous enough under normal circumstances, but with a strong wind fanning the furnace it was lethal. The steam pressure rapidly built up until the boiler was no longer able to withstand the mounting stresses, and there was an enormous explosion. The blast threw Corner 16 yards, breaking his thigh. After the accident, George Stephenson's friend, mathematician and inventor Thomas Brandreth, presented Corner with half a sovereign in compensation. Gillespie received one whole sovereign, but he died from his wounds before he had a chance to spend it. James Stephenson escaped uninjured, and because there was no inquiry, no blame was ever attached to him. Apparently no lessons were learned, either by the company or by the drivers, for July 1 that year saw another boiler explosion on the line, this time involving near-sister engine *Locomotion No.1*, which in 1825 had become the first steam locomotive to haul a passenger train on a public railway, and had been built by Robert Stephenson & Co. in 1824. The boiler exploded at Aycliffe Lane station, killing driver John Cree, after the safety valves had been left fixed down while the engine was stationary. It was rebuilt and remained in service until 1841 when it was turned into a stationary engine. It is now preserved as a static exhibit in Head of Steam, the museum at Darlington's North Road station.

THE SEMINAL DAY THAT TURNED SOUR

In 1829, the Liverpool & Manchester Railway held the Rainhill Trials, not only to see which of the entrants' steam locomotives was the best – *Rocket* won the day – but to establish a more fundamental principle – was the steam locomotive, as opposed to the horse or cable haulage – the future of motive power? By the time the railway opened, on September 6, 1830, that principle had been effectively cast in stone. Now, for the first time, two major cities were to be linked by a steam railway. Britain and the world would never be the same again. It was not only a watershed in the development of transport, but a major landmark in world history. On the day of the official opening, enormous crowds flocked to Liverpool to watch the trains depart, at Sankey Valley to watch them pass over the viaduct, and to Manchester to watch them arrive. Near Sankey Viaduct, a grandstand had been erected for 1,000 people, and a ticket to enter cost 10s 6d; a fortune in those days. The roads approaching Liverpool had for several days beforehand been packed with visitors pouring into the port to attend the event, while others arrived by ship from Scotland and Ireland. Every hotel room and lodging-house in Liverpool was full the night before. From 9am onwards the area around the station was filled with onlookers.

City-centre streets were packed to capacity, as everyone made their way to their chosen vantage point. At Edge Hill locomotive depot, several men climbed up the inside of the chimneys to get a better view from the top, while others climbed up a nearby windmill. One group of men each paid two shillings for access to the best vantage point of all; the top of the air shaft of the tunnel leading to Crown Street station. They were hoisted up by a rope and board shortly after dawn for their private grandstand view. The chief guest was the Tory Prime Minister, Arthur Wellesley, the first Duke of Wellington, who had agreed to open the railway. Three special carriages had been built for the occasion, with the most magnificent of them for the Duke. Just before 10am as the Duke arrived, a band played *See, the Conquering Hero Comes* in praise of his victory over Napoleon at Waterloo. The rendition started a tradition of the song being played at almost every British railway station opening from then on. The Duke's party boarded their carriage before a gun was then fired to mark the official opening of the railway. The carriages of the Duke's train had their brakes released and were allowed to roll down the incline under the force of gravity to be coupled to the waiting locomotive at the bottom. Soldiers cleared onlookers from the tracks before a procession of trains left Crown Street station at 11am, all on time and without any technical problems. The Duke's special train ran on one track, with the other seven trains operating on a parallel track, sometimes running ahead and sometimes behind the Duke's train. *Northumbrian*, the last of the *Rocket*-style 0-2-2s, hauled the Duke's train, driven by George Stephenson. The others were led by No. 6 *Phoenix*, driven by George's son Robert.

The first mishap of the day occurred 13 miles out of Liverpool. One of the trains derailed and the train behind collided with it. The concept of train paths and leaving sufficient distance between them was still very much in an embryonic stage. Thankfully, this time there were no injuries or damage. *Phoenix*, the derailed locomotive, was re-railed and continued its journey. Again, history, albeit unwanted, was made on the day – the first collision between two passenger trains. The locomotives stopped at the midway point of Parkside station, half a mile east of Newton-le-Willows and 17 miles from Liverpool, to take on water, 55 minutes after departure. Railway officials told passengers to stay on board while the engines' tanks were replenished, but this instruction was quickly forgotten when the special train carrying the Duke of Wellington also stopped, and about 50 of the VIPs alighted. Huskisson, who had done so much over several years to make the Liverpool & Manchester Railway a reality, had felt it was his duty to attend the opening day, despite still recovering from serious illness.

A highly influential figure in the creation of the British Empire and an architect of the doctrine of free trade, Huskisson had fallen out with Wellington in 1828 over the issue of parliamentary reform and resigned from the cabinet. However, he hoped on the day that the pair might become friends again. He approached wealthy Liverpool corn merchant Joseph Sandars, one of the original promoters of the railway. After congratulating Sandars on the realisation of his vision, saying that he, "must be one of the happiest men in the world," William Holmes, the Tory Chief Whip, called Huskisson to one side. Holmes said that the Duke was in a particularly good mood thanks to the cheering crowds lining the route, and it might be an opportune moment for him to attempt reconciliation. Newspapers of the day were reporting rumours that Huskisson and his supporters were to be invited back into the government. Accordingly, Huskisson approached the Duke's carriage and shook his hand. Huskisson was so elated at his positive reception by the Prime Minister that he did not notice that *Rocket* was approaching on the parallel track. Bystanders shouted to alert those standing on the tracks. "An engine is approaching, take care gentlemen," they yelled. Engineer Joseph Locke, who was driving *Rocket*, saw that there were people on the line ahead. He could not slam on the brakes – because there weren't any. *Rocket* was an engineering prototype, and had not been equipped with brakes. So, Locke threw the engine into reverse gear, a process that took 10 seconds.

Huskisson and Holmes realised the danger too late and panicked. Holmes clung to the side of the Duke's carriage, but after making two vain attempts to run across the tracks to safety, Huskisson found himself pressed against the side of the carriage. The Duke is said to have told Huskisson: "We seem to be going on – you had better step in!" Huskisson tried to clamber into the carriage, but the passengers inside failed to reach him to pull him in. Holmes was still outside the carriage and was said to have shouted: "For God's sake, Mr Huskisson, be firm." The Duke's carriage had not been fitted with fixed steps, and relied on a portable set fixed to the rear. Huskisson misjudged the distance and grabbed the handle of the carriage door, but it swung open leaving him hanging directly in the path of the oncoming locomotive.

Rocket collided with the door and Huskisson fell on to the tracks in front of the oncoming train, suffering extremely serious leg injuries. It was reported that he exclaimed: "I have met my death – God forgive me!" Tory diarist Harriet Arbuthnot, a friend of the Duke who was riding in his carriage, wrote that the MP, "was caught by it, thrown down and the engine passed over his leg and thigh, crushing it in a most frightful way." It is impossible to give an idea of the scene that followed, of the horror of everyone present or of the piercing shrieks of his unfortunate wife, who was in the car. He said scarcely more than: "It's all over with me. Bring me my wife and let me die." Had Huskisson stayed where he was when he saw *Rocket* approaching, he would have been safe, but it was his panic that led to his death. Men raced along the track in both directions to warn the other trains not to proceed and amid the scenes of panic, it was first thought that the Duke had been assassinated.

THE WORLD'S FIRST AMBULANCE TRAIN

Northumbrian was hastily detached from the special to take Huskisson to hospital, in doing so, forming the world's first ambulance train, which reached a speed of 35mph. The dying MP was carried to the vicarage at Eccles and placed in the care of the wife of the vicar, Rev. Thomas Blackburne, while George Stephenson drove *Northumbrian* on to Manchester with Lord Wilton, after uncoupling the trailing musicians' carriage, and collecting four surgeons – who returned to Eccles riding on the tender. Sadly, despite the best efforts that could be made on the spot, the MP died in the vicarage at 8.45pm after changing his will in favour of his wife Emily, who witnessed much of the tragedy. The Duke and Home Secretary, Sir Robert Peel, took the view that the remainder of the day's events should be cancelled out of respect to Huskisson, and proposed to return to Liverpool. Yet by then a large crowd had gathered in Manchester to see the trains arrive, and was beginning to become unruly. They clearly would have had none of it.

To appease them and prevent disturbances, Wellington was persuaded to continue to Manchester. The compromise reached was to cancel the festivities and send the military bands home, while carrying on with the train journeys as best they could. However, by the time the trains reached the outskirts of Manchester, the crowd had become hostile as the Duke was becoming unpopular as Prime Minister, particularly in the industrial North-

West, for persistently blocking reforms. There were those in the crowd who had set out to make the celebrations a day of political protest, with the tricolour flag of revolution draped from several bridges. There were shouts in protest against the lack of secret ballots for voting, and the Corn Laws. The authorities found themselves to be powerless to clear the line, and so the trains had to proceed at very low speed into the crowd. They relied on their own momentum to push people out of the way. It was reported that a mob from Oldham was on the warpath. Around 50 special constables were gathered and armed with staves and clubs to guard the railway. Another rumour about a mob riot, which proved baseless, led to a troop of dragoons being despatched from Manchester. Eventually, the trains reached the Liverpool Road terminus. An even more hostile crowd was waiting there. They waved banners and flags in protest against the Duke and pelted his train with vegetables.

Wellington refused to disembark, but shook hands through the windows with Tory supporters who had turned out to see him, and were not among those protesting. After 90 minutes, the head of the local police urged that the trains return to Liverpool before the crowds reached the point where there would be no way through them. An inability to turn the locomotives and a failure of one that had already returned to Liverpool meant that most of the trains were unable to leave Manchester. While Wellington's train left successfully, only three of the remaining seven locomotives were usable. These three locomotives slowly hauled a single long train of 24 carriages back to Liverpool, eventually arriving 6½ hours late after having been pelted with objects thrown from bridges by the drunken crowds lining the track. When the train reached Liverpool, people who had just heard about the fate of their MP surrounded it. The crowds dispersed after the Duke left, while the train was still on its way. While ascending the Sutton incline, the train stopped and fell back under its own weight as the five locomotives were not powerful enough to stop it.

Around 400 men alighted and walked up the incline to reduce the load. After the train restarted from the top of the incline, it came to a halt after locomotive *Comet* collided with a wheelbarrow that had been placed across the tracks. Passing through Rainhill, more miscreants, who had been drinking all day, pelted it with missiles. Finally, it arrived at Wapping at 10.30pm.

CELEBRATIONS TURNED TO GRIEF

In view of Huskisson's death, the engineers' banquet that night and the celebratory ball the following evening were cancelled. The company held a dinner for 219 guests at the Wellington Rooms, but only 47 turned up, and left after drinking to the late MP. A VIP party including the Duke were given a guided tour through the Edge Hill tunnel the following day. However, earlier that day, he had written to the city mayor turning down the Freedom of the City, which he had been due to receive, out of respect to Huskisson. The next day, a coroner's jury was hastily assembled in the Grapes pub in Eccles. Lord Granville, the half-brother of the Marquess of Stafford, told the hearing that Huskisson had been suffering from numbness in his leg from a previous operation, and that this may have caused problems with movement when he tried to dodge *Rocket*.

No witnesses remembered seeing any signal flags raised from any of the locomotives involved during the day, including *Rocket*, although a system of warning flags was supposed to have been in place. Some eyewitnesses said that Locke had been at fault. However, after the coroner addressed the jury, a verdict of accidental death was returned, and the railway officials were absolved of any blame. Nonetheless, the following year George Stephenson insisted that any new locomotives bought by the railway were to be fitted with handbrakes. Emily Huskisson found two speeches in her husband's jacket pocket, the first being a brief tribute to James Watt, the inventor of the condensing steam engine. The second talked about the benefits of railways: "...the principle of a Railway is that of commerce itself – it multiplies the enjoyment of Mankind by increasing the facilities and diminishing the labour by which [goods] are produced and distributed throughout the world."

Huskisson's funeral was held on Friday, September 24, 1830. Around 1,100 citizens of Liverpool formed a procession in front of road carriages carrying aristocrats and other VIPs. Behind the city mayor's state carriage walked another 900 Liverpudlians and a further nine coaches. Every pub in Liverpool was closed. It was estimated that around 69,000, about half the city's population, lined the route of the funeral procession. Ecstasy had turned to grief. One diarist wrote: "Can it be that these terrible Monsters will ever come into general use?" Yes, it could, and certainly would, within days.

Two months after the opening of the railway, the Duke lost a vote of no confidence and was replaced as Prime Minister a week later by Earl Grey, who brought in electoral reforms that had been supported by Huskisson, leading to the 1832 Reform Act.
The Duke remained opposed to railways for the rest of his life because they would, "encourage the lower classes to travel about." However, in 1843 he accompanied Queen Victoria on a trip on the London & South Western Railway – which had been designed by Locke. Emily Huskisson died in 1856, never again having travelled by train. The death and funeral of William Huskisson was understandably a cause of great mourning, yet inadvertently boosted the railway's publicity. It served to reinforce the fact to people across the world that cheap and rapid long-distance transport was now possible. There's no such thing as bad publicity.

On the afternoon of September 15, the day after the official opening, the railway started a regular scheduled service. The monument beneath which Huskisson is buried is the centrepiece of St James Cemetery in Liverpool. A marble statue of him was housed in a specially built mausoleum there until 1968, when it was transferred to the Walker Art Gallery in Liverpool. Emily also commissioned a second marble statue for the Custom House in Liverpool. This statue now stands in Pimlico Gardens in London. Using the second marble sculpture as a master, a bronze version was cast and unveiled in October 1847. Its original location was in front of the Customs House in Canning Place, Liverpool, but was destroyed during Second World War air raids. In 1954 the sculpture was moved to a new home on the Princes Road/ Princes Avenue boulevard. However, it was pulled from its plinth in the Toxteth Riots of 1981 because people wrongly thought that Huskisson had been a slave trader. From 1982 onwards the bronze sculpture was housed in the Oratory in St James Mount Gardens. In 2004 it was taken into the sculpture studios at the National Conservation Centre for conservation and is now located in Duke Street Terrace, a housing development off Duke Street in the city centre. There is a monument of him by Carew in Chichester Cathedral (he was elected as MP for Chichester in 1830). In 1800 Huskisson bought Eartham House in West Sussex from his friend William Hayley, and is commemorated in the parish church by a long carved eulogy from Emily on the south wall.

OTHERS WHO SHOULD HAVE KNOWN BETTER
Following Huskisson's death, brakes were added to steam locomotives. Huskisson may be regarded by many as the first fatal railway victim by walking on the lines of a public railway, but he would never be the last. Maybe he should have known better, having done so much to help promote the railway and having seen locomotives in action. Yet from

then until now, trespassing by members of the public on railways is a perennial problem. That is one reason why all railways must be fenced off by law.

On February 25, 2016, the world's most famous steam locomotive, A3 Pacific No. 60103 (LNER 4472) *Flying Scotsman*, made its long-awaited comeback following a 10-year overhaul that cost owner the National Railway Museum upwards of £4 million. With tickets priced at £450 a seat, the locomotive headed its comeback trip from King's Cross to York in the glare of global media. Tens of thousands of people turned out along the route to glimpse and photograph this great celebrity locomotive as it sped past in glorious sunshine. Bridges, fields, tops of embankments, station platforms, were all packed with sightseers. One lady was even seen standing on top of a farmyard manure heap to get the best view possible. On two occasions, one south of Peterborough and the other when the train was brought to a halt by the presence of spectators who had disregarded fences and strayed on to the lineside, people were regardless or oblivious to the colossal danger. Their actions caused several regular main line services also to be delayed.

Exactly the same happened on July 4, 1999, *Flying Scotsman*'s previous return to service after it was rebuilt by then owner, the late pharmaceuticals entrepreneur Dr. Tony Marchington. I witnessed at various points people standing next to the ballast at several points on the line, including one father with a toddler perched on his shoulders. We now live in a celebrity culture, and it seems when you have the chance to glimpse a celebrity, normally human but in this case mechanical, cares can be cast to the wind. Many of those bystanders probably have neither any railway knowledge nor awareness of safety hazards, or even the slightest interest in steam railways normally, but simply turned out to see something famous. You can arrest and fine people for railway trespass. You can go into schools and preach about the dangers to life and limb about walking on railways. You can show advertisements on TV. You can sound warnings on station tannoys and add warning notices ad infinitum. But still they come.

Arguably the most glaring example of a man who should have known better is Great Western Railway Chief Mechanical Engineer, George Jackson Churchward, widely regarded as the finest and arguably the most influential of all British locomotive engineers. His GWR designs set the pace for many of those that followed in the 20th century, right up to the last days of steam under British Railways. Through his efforts, the GWR became regarded as a symbol of excellence, a railway that was the envy of the world, which many others tried to follow. His first design, the 20-strong City class of 4-4-0s, has become the stuff of legend. On May 9, 1904, No. 3440 *City of Truro* laid its unofficial claim to being the first steam locomotive to break the 100mph barrier, while descending Wellington Bank in Somerset with the 'Ocean Mails Special' from Plymouth to Paddington. Churchward retired in 1922, handing over the reins to Charles B. Collett. Churchward, who never married, died on December 19, 1933, at the age of 75 – after being run over by a GWR steam locomotive. In his retirement he still visited Swindon Works, and was walking there from his home in thick fog when he stepped across the tracks. He was inspecting a defective sleeper when he was hit by a Paddington to Fishguard express, hauled by Collett 4-6-0 No. 4085 *Berkeley Castle*, the Castle class being his successor's innovated derivative of Churchward's Stars.

Chapter 2

1833 BAGWORTH: THE INTRODUCTION OF THE FIRST WHISTLES?

According to some accounts, an engine colliding with a horse and cart led to the introduction of one of the most distinctive features of a steam locomotive – its whistle! It is astonishing that Stephenson's *Rocket*, despite its many mechanical innovations, did not have brakes when Liverpool MP William Huskisson was killed in 1830. Neither did early locomotives have warning whistles. Five locomotives were built by Robert Stephenson & Co. for the Liverpool and Manchester Railway. The first was 0-4-0 *Comet*, its first trip being on the opening day in 1830, when its 13ft-high chimney was said to have been knocked down by Glenfield Tunnel. The second engine, *Phoenix*, was delivered in 1832 and sold in 1835 for use on the construction of the London & Birmingham Railway. The next were *Samson* and *Goliath*, delivered in 1833. They were initially 0-4-0s, but were extremely unstable and a pair of trailing wheels was added. This 0-4-2 formation was also used for the fifth engine, *Hercules*. These were the first six-wheeled goods engines with inside cylinders and, after the flanges were taken off the centre pair of wheels, were so satisfactory, that Robert Stephenson never built another four-wheeled engine.

It is said that *Samson* collided with either a horse and cart or a herd of cows at Thornton level crossing near Bagworth on its way to Leicester market with a trainload of butter and eggs. Although no one was injured, the incident was considered serious. Although *Samson* had a horn, which was sounded by driver Weatherburn, it was not loud enough, and the company manager, Ashlin Bagster, suggested that a horn or whistle that could be activated by steam should be constructed and fixed to the locomotives.

George Stephenson invented and patented a 'steam trumpet' for use on the line after calling a meeting of the railway's directors. A copy of the trumpet drawing signed May 1833 shows a device about 18in high with an ever-widening trumpet shape with a 6in diameter at its top or mouth. He visited a musical instrument maker in Leicester's Duke Street and instructed him to build the trumpet, which was tested in his presence 10 days later. Stephenson mounted the trumpet on the top of the boiler's steam dome, which delivered dry steam to the cylinders. The company went on to mount the device on its other engines. The idea caught on very rapidly, although steam whistles soon replaced locomotive steam trumpets. However, author C.R. Clinker has cast doubt on the accuracy of this story, or indeed whether it happened at all. In his account of the Leicester & Swannington Railway, he stated that while minutes of directors' meetings recorded some trivial accidents, there was no mention of this particular accident, nor of any records of payments made for claims for damages or to a 'musical instrument maker'. Trade directories of Leicester for the time do not include an instrument maker in Duke Street.

Chapter 3

1865 STAPLEHURST: HEROISM OF
OUR MUTUAL FRIEND

Novelist Charles Dickens, one of the world's best-loved authors, was a passenger in a train which crashed on a viaduct at Staplehurst in Kent, after workmen told nobody that they had removed a length of track on it. Ten people died; the writer tended to the wounded and dying, and then ran back inside the wrecked train to rescue his latest manuscript. On Friday, June 9, 1865, the South Eastern Railway's daily boat train to London left Folkestone just before 2.40pm, having taken on board passengers from the tidal cross-channel ferry from France. The service, headed on this occasion by SER tender locomotive No. 199, one of the famous Cudworth singles with 7ft diameter driving wheels, was often referred to as the 'tidal train'. Packed with continental pleasure-seekers, it comprised a brake van, a second-class carriage, seven first-class carriages, two more second-class carriages and three more brake vans, carrying in all 80 first-class and 35 second-class passengers. Three of the brake vans contained a guard and these were able to communicate with the driver using a whistle on the engine.

Shortly after the train passed Headcorn station at 45-50mph, the driver saw a red flag. He whistled for the brakes and reversed his engine, but the locomotive and brakesmen were unable to stop the train before it derailed at 3.13pm while crossing the 10ft-high River Beult viaduct at Staplehurst. There, unknown to the train crew, a length of track had been removed during engineering works on the viaduct, with inevitable consequences. The 10ft-high viaduct spanned a riverbed, which was mostly dry at the time of the accident. The train jumped the rails before splitting into two. The locomotive, tender, a van and a second-class carriage made it across and remained coupled to a first-class carriage, the other end of which rested in the dry river-bed. The next seven carriages ended up in the mud and the last second-class carriage remained coupled to the trailing vans, the last two of which remained on the eastern bank. Ten people died and 40 others were seriously injured while seven carriages were destroyed.

Inside a first-class coach left hanging over the bridge with its rear end resting on the field below were novelist Charles Dickens, his mistress Ellen Ternan and her mother Frances Ternan, all returning to London from a month in Paris. Ellen's presence was a guilty secret that Dickens was concealing from his adoring public, and he now found himself in a predicament that came very close to exposing that secret. We do not know why Dickens chose to travel in the front carriage as it was an unpopular location with travellers at the time as the first and last carriages were the most likely to be destroyed in the event of a crash. Maybe he felt that the brake van in front of his coach would absorb any impact. Nonetheless, Dickens played a significant part in the subsequent rescue efforts. Despite sustaining minor injuries himself, he climbed out of a window, and noticed two guards running up and down. He summoned them and, with their help, used planks to lead the Ternans out of the carriage and to safety. He helped them up the bank and returned to the carriage. Once back inside, he retrieved his top hat and a flask of brandy. Filling the hat with water, he scrambled down the bank and started to tend the other victims, some of whom died while he was with them. He administered brandy to a man with a severely cracked skull and a woman propped against a tree, but he could not save either.

Before he left with other survivors in an emergency train to Charing Cross station, to the utter astonishment of the survivors and onlookers, he returned to the carriage, which was then tottering on the brink, and retrieved the manuscript of *Our Mutual Friend*. He acknowledged the incident in the novel's postscript: "On Friday the Ninth of June in the present year, Mr and Mrs Boffin (in their manuscript dress of receiving Mr and Mrs Lammle at breakfast) were on the South Eastern Railway with me, in a terribly destructive accident. When I had done what I could to help others, I climbed back into my carriage – nearly turned over a viaduct, and caught aslant upon the turn — to extricate the worthy couple. They were much soiled, but otherwise unhurt. I remember with devout thankfulness that I can never be much nearer parting company with my readers forever than I was then, until there shall be written against my life, the two words with which I have this day closed this book: – THE END." *Our Mutual Friend* is now regarded as one of Dickens' greatest works, so his final heroic act on the day saved a priceless piece of English literature.

Afterwards Dickens was nervous when travelling by train, using alternative means when available. SER directors later presented Dickens with a piece of plate as a token of their appreciation for his assistance. Dickens was greatly affected by the tragedy, losing his voice for two weeks, and shaking so much that he could not write for a week. He remained resolute that he would not attend the subsequent inquest into the disaster, most likely because it would mean revealing that he had been travelling with Ellen Ternan. However, soon afterwards he wrote a short story, a ghost story named *The Signalman*, in which one of the main incidents is a rail crash in a tunnel. A 1976 BBC dramatisation of the story was filmed on the Severn Valley Railway. Dickens died on the exact fifth anniversary of the accident, leaving *The Mystery of Edwin Drood* unfinished, his son claiming that he had never fully recovered from his experience at Staplehurst.

PENAL RETRIBUTION AND PERMANENT PROTECTION
The Board of Trade report into the disaster, published on June 21, 1865, found that for the previous eight to ten weeks, a team of eight men and a foreman had been renewing the timbers under the track on viaducts between Headcorn and Staplehurst stations. The track would be removed when no train was due; however, on June 9, the foreman had misread his timetable and there had also been no notification to the driver about the track repairs. A man had been placed with a red flag 554 yards away, but the regulations required him to be 1,000 yards away. Accordingly, the train did not have enough time to stop. It later transpired that Henry Benge, the foreman of the worker gang, consulted the wrong timetable and so was not expecting the boat train for another two hours. Also, he did not issue sufficient detonators to platelayer's labourer John Wiles, whose duty it was to place detonators on the track at 250-yard intervals, up to 1,000 yards, to explode under the wheels of any unexpected train and warn the driver of danger. Benge also instructed that the detonators were not to be placed on the track unless visibility was poor. As it was a bright sunny afternoon, the detonators were not placed. Benge was found guilty by a grand jury of culpable negligence of passenger Hannah Cunliff and was sentenced to nine months' imprisonment.

At 3.13pm, on Tuesday, June 9, 2015, members of the Staplehurst Society marked the 150th anniversary of the crash, visiting the location to remember the victims. Anita Thompson read out the names of those who had perished and, at the appropriate minute, a colourful wreath was cast, from the river bank, to float on the river a few yards from the site of the derailment. It had not been possible to access the exact spot owing to recent necessary alterations to the river by the local water company. It has been said that the Staplehurst accident led to, or at least contributed to, the formation of Rule 55, Protection of Train, which is still in use in a much-modified form today. The basic principle is that waiting trains on running lines must remind the signal controller (signaller) of their presence. Staplehurst apart, Rule 55 was introduced following a spate of accidents caused by signalmen forgetting that trains were standing on a running line, sometimes within sight of their signal boxes. It applied on British railways in the 19th and 20th centuries, and was superseded by the Modular Rulebook following privatisation.

Chapter 4

1868 ABERGELE: INFERNO OF
THE IRISH MAIL

Not only was the collision on the North Wales Coast Line at Abergele on August 20, 1868, the worst railway disaster in Britain to that point in history, but was also considered the most horrific. Thirty-three people lost their lives in an inferno when the London & North Western Railway's Irish Mail express crashed into a rake of runaway petrol tank wagons. The express left Euston for Holyhead slightly late on August 20, 1868, behind Lady of the Lake class 2-2-2 No. 291 *Prince of Wales.*

The train comprised a chief guard's van, a travelling post office, a luggage van, four passenger carriages, and a second guard's van at the back. Four more passenger coaches were added at Chester. It was about five minutes late by the time it passed through the seaside town of Abergele. Ahead of it, a 42-wagon pick-up goods train had left Abergele at 12.15pm, and was to be temporarily shunted into one of two sidings at Llandulas, three miles away, to allow the Irish Mail express to pass.

The goods train reached the two sidings around 12.25pm, but they were partly occupied by freight wagons so neither siding could take the entire train. Under the direction of the Llandulas station master, therefore, the brake van and last six wagons of the goods train were uncoupled and left on the main Down line, but protected by the Distant signal for Llandulas. He could have chosen to shunt the rest of the train into one of the sidings and return for the odd six. Instead, a series of loose shunting operations were begun with the aim of placing the 26 empty wagons into one siding and assembling a shorter rake of loaded wagons on the main line to go into the other sidings. Both brakesmen on the freight alighted to take part in the shunting, leaving the wagons held only by the brake van, on a gradient as steep as 1-in-100, falling towards Abergele. A set of loaded wagons was loose shunted into the first set of wagons with such force that the unsecured brake in the brake van was released by the impact.

The ingredients for a perfect storm were in place. The wagons began rolling down the gradient towards Abergele, and nobody was manning the brake van, so the brake could not be reapplied. The first plan was to reverse the goods train engine and retrieve the runaway wagons. But it was too late. Arthur Thompson, the driver of *Prince of Wales*, was 1¾ miles out of Abergele when he saw the wagons rolling towards his locomotive 200 yards away. At first he thought they were on the Up line, but then realised to his horror they were on the same line as him. Travelling at up to 30mph, Thompson shut off steam, and his fireman applied the locomotive brake, but in vain. The wagons were running at up to 15mph. A collision was inevitable. The sheer force of the impact derailed *Prince of Wales*, its tender and the guard's van leading the Irish Mail. The locomotive ran on over the ballast and sleepers for about 30 yards before overturning. The collision was not so much the problem as the load carried by the wagons. The pair next to the brake van were carrying 1,700 gallons of paraffin oil between them in 50 wooden barrels. Several barrels were shattered by the impact, and the paraffin oil caught fire. *Prince of Wales*, its tender, guard's van and first three passenger coaches were instantly shrouded in a cloud of dense smoke and flames.

The fire quickly set the fourth carriage and the front of the leading post office van ablaze, making it impossible to rescue the passengers in the first four carriages. The locked carriage doors prevented escape, and 28 of the 33 victims burned to death. Among the deaths were the fireman, the guard in the front guard's van and the Irish Mail fireman, Joe Holmes. Driver Thompson survived the crash although wounded. He died in October the same year from ulcerated bowels, which he had suffered from before, but an inquest decided that his death had been hastened by his injuries. Workers in the travelling post office escaped along with some of the mail, but the leading post office van was gutted. Nobody in the vehicles behind the post van was killed or even seriously injured, and the remaining coaches were detached and saved. A first-class passenger and local labourers were despatched by foot to Llandulas, and the Up Irish Mail was held there. Farm labourers and quarry workers numbering more than 100 in all formed a bucket chain to carry sea water from the shore to extinguish the burning carriages. When the fire was out, those inside the carriages were found to have been burned so badly that three of them could be identified only by personal belongings. Eventually, three parties of LNWR workmen, from Crewe, Chester and Holyhead, arrived to take over.

THE DRIVER'S TALE

Driver Thompson told the *Illustrated London News* that he had not seen the wagons until his train was within a few yards of them, and, seeing that there were barrels of oil on board, he resolved at once to jump off the engine. Before leaping, he said to fireman Holmes, "Joe, jump off." Thompson jumped off on the embankment side and landed on his feet. However, he was struck by a fragment of the guard's van, next to the tender, which threw him down on the embankment. He rose to his feet again, suffering from wounds in the head, hand and knee, and saw that the tender had gone right over the engine, and that the van and foremost carriages were on fire. He ran to the back carriages, assisted in uncoupling them from the rest of the train, and handed a carriage key to a tall gentleman who was standing on the steps of a carriage. In an instant after Thompson had handed him the key, he observed that the carriage on the steps of which the man had been standing was ablaze. He never saw that man again.

He heard a cry from under the engine, which he believed to have been uttered by his fireman. Thompson said that the fire spread from carriage to carriage with the rapidity of lightning, and that there was no going near one once it had caught fire. He and other witnesses said that not a cry came from anyone in the blazing carriages, and that no one in any of them made an attempt to get out. It was thought they were suffocated by the fumes of the burning petroleum, or stunned by the explosion. *The Railway News* commented: "No other collision has ever yet, in this country at least, been attended with such a loss of life, nor presented such horrifying features. The crashing of the engine and carriages into a heap of splinters, each of which wounds unfortunate passengers like a sword, is horrible enough to contemplate; but when fire in its fiercest form is added to the scene, no more frightful occurrence could be imagined."

A PASSENGER'S ACCOUNT

One of the passengers, the Marquis of Hamilton, eldest son of the Duke of Abercorn, Lord Lieutenant of Ireland, said: "We were startled by a collision and a shock which, though not very severe, was sufficient to throw everyone against his opposite neighbour. I immediately jumped out of the carriage, when a fearful sight met my view. Already the whole of the three passenger carriages in front of ours, the vans, and the engine were enveloped in dense sheets of flame and smoke, rising fully 20ft high and spreading out in every direction; it was the work of an instant. No words can convey the instantaneous nature of the explosion and conflagration. I had actually got out almost before the shock of the collision was over, and this was the spectacle which already presented itself. Not a sound, not a scream, not a struggle to escape, or a movement of any sort was apparent in the doomed carriages. It was as though an electric flash had at once paralysed and stricken every one of their occupants." The surviving passengers carried on their journey at 6pm the same day, when the Up Irish Mail proceeded as planned.

Nine days later, the *Illustrated London News* reported: "A new horror has been added to the number of horrors to which railway travellers are exposed. A rush down the crater of Mount Vesuvius into the fiery gulf beneath it could hardly be more appalling. A momentary crash – a dense cloud, blacker than night, of suffocating vapour – an all-enwrapping, all-consuming flame of fire – and between 30 and 40 human beings, comprising old and young, noble and simple, all rejoicing but a minute before in life and its pleasures, most of them probably gazing with delight upon the picturesque scene through which they were passing, were transformed into a heap of charred and undistinguishable remains. Death and destruction overwhelmed them in an instant, leaving to their surviving relatives scarcely a memorial of their former existence. What passed in the thoughts and feelings of the victims, between the first revelation of danger and the last pulsation of life, it were better not to imagine. We ask, what were the causes of this awful calamity? Were they preventable by ordinary care, or were they wholly beyond the range of human foresight? Are we to regard the tragic occurrence as entirely exceptional, or must we for the future reckon death by fire as one of the liabilities of passengers by the rail? The accident comes fearfully close to home to every one of us, and much of our future confidence and comfort in travelling will depend upon the results of the investigation which the event has made indispensable."

ACCUSED AND ACQUITTED: THE TWO BRAKESMEN
Investigating on behalf of the Board of Trade, Colonel Frederick Henry Rich, the chief inspecting officer of the Railway Inspectorate between 1885-89, produced a report within a month of the Abergele disaster. He said that the immediate cause of the accident was the failure of the senior brakesman to apply the individual wagon brakes on the six detached wagons. Furthermore, the colonel found that the brake van brake had been broken by loose shunting of loaded wagons at too high a speed. The secondary cause was the failure of the senior brakesman to moderate the wagons' speed by applying wagon brakes. He also reported that the Llandulas station master was very culpable in not having directed the goods train into the sidings as soon as it arrived. He also said that the LNWR was to blame to some extent, as well as its staff on the ground. The colonel wrote: "So far, the three men are seriously to blame, and their neglect has been the immediate cause of the accident, but men of that class cannot be expected to do their duties well if the railway companies do not give them the most convenient and best appliances, and do not look after them strictly and enforce their own regulations." He criticised the LNWR for operating the section of line on the interval system, with intervals between trains seeming wholly inadequate, and that the block telegraph system should be installed at this location and others like it. He continued that Llandulas station and the sidings had never been inspected by a government official or been approved by the Board of Trade, and were "quite unfit" to be used to support both local quarry operations and house slower trains when expresses needed to pass them. He recommended that an additional siding large enough to accommodate any train being passed should be provided, while being kept free from quarry traffic.

He said that the LNWR, "appeared to have a very slack system of supervision," with nobody to look after guards, train them, or monitor their performance. He recommended that dangerous materials should be sent in special trains and not included in normal goods trains. The colonel also recommended that all carriage doors should be left unlocked, as opposed to being locked from the outside, as was the case here. He concluded: "I must disavow any intention of taking advantage of this sad calamity to be severe on the London & North Western Railway Company. I believe that their line is one of the best in the country, and that its general management and arrangements are as good, on the whole, as those of any of the other lines. But I desire to take advantage of the attention which this deplorable event will attract to bring before railway companies what I conceive to be the great defect in their systems, which has led to most of the accidents I have inquired into, viz a want of discipline and the enforcing of obedience to their own rules."

At the resulting inquest, the coroner's jury returned a verdict of manslaughter against the two goods train brakesmen, who, after taking legal advice, did not give evidence. Furthermore, the jury strongly censured the Llandulas station master for flouting company rules by allowing shunting when the express was expected imminently. The pair were sent to Ruthin Assizes the following spring to stand trial. The judge indicated that the brakesmen were, or should have been, under the control of a superior officer, the station master, and therefore it was up to the jury to decide whose negligence had caused the accident. The trial jury was out for less than 10 minutes before returning a not-guilty verdict. The colonel's recommendation about dangerous substances would not be enacted upon in law for another 11 years. In 1879, the Petroleum Act finally regulated the carriage of flammable liquids by rail. Although the colonel did not list it in his recommendations, in the wake of the Abergele disaster it became the practice for steep gradients to be equipped with runaway catch points. Had this been the case here, the catch points would have derailed the wagons before they hit the Irish Mail. Catch points hereafter became a universal feature of the UK network, until the 1980s when all rolling stock was fitted with continuous automatic brakes.

Chapter 5

1874 THORPE: WHY EDWARD TYER INVENTED THE TABLET SYSTEM

Ten people died in a head-on collision at Thorpe St Andrew in Norfolk on September 10, 1874 – but a telecommunications expert, who set out to ensure the same mistakes could not be made again, went on to save countless lives. The trains were the 8.40pm mail from Yarmouth and the 5pm 14-coach express from London to Yarmouth, and collided on what was a single-track line between Norwich and Brundall. The express had left Norwich Thorpe at 9.30pm and would normally have had a clear run on its way to Yarmouth, with the mail train being held on a loop line at Brundall to allow the express to pass. However, on this evening, both were running late. In such circumstances, when the timetable had effectively gone out of the window, locomotive drivers had to obtain written authority to proceed. Yet in this case, the telegraph clerk sent the authorisation message before it had been signed by the appropriate official, and this mistake was compounded by several misunderstandings also involving the station master and the night inspector. Both drivers received the necessary authority, and, mindful of the need to make up for lost time, sped off along the single track. It was at 9.45pm when they realised that mistakes had been made with the authorisation, and collision was unavoidable.

Contemporary newspaper reports described it as the worst head-on collision in the history of British railways. The rails were slippery from rain, there was a slight curve in the line at the fatal spot, so that the lights of neither train could be seen, there was no time to apply the brakes, and the two engines rushed at each other at full speed. The locomotive drawing the mail train, No. 54, was said to be "of the most approved modern construction and of great power" and was thought to have been travelling at 35mph. The engine drawing the train from Norwich was a lighter one, but had acquired, with its train, a considerable momentum before the impact, and was travelling at around 25mph. "Imagination can only faintly conceive the fearful shock of two such bodies propelled with this velocity, each presenting exactly the same points of contact, and giving and receiving at the same instant the full force of each other's blow," commented the *Illustrated London News*.

Both locomotives were raised into the air by the sheer force of the collision, the funnel of engine No. 54 was carried away. The engine from Norwich ended up on top of No. 54, the carriages of each train following, until a pyramid was formed of the stock. Both sets of drivers and firemen were killed, along with 17 passengers. Four more passengers died later from their injuries, while 73 others and two railway guards were seriously injured. The accident, which happened yards away from a wooden bridge over the River Yare, would probably have been far worse if it had occurred on the bridge itself. Had the wrecked carriages tumbled into the water, it is almost certain that the death toll would have been far higher.

A LIFESAVER BORN OUT OF TRAGEDY

Board of Trade inspector Captain Tyler's official report apportioned the blame between night inspector Cooper and telegraph clerk Robson, and criticised the laxity of the system that allowed such mistakes to occur. However, a solution was at hand. Prompted by the Thorpe accident, engineer Edward Tyer developed the tablet system in which a token is given to the train driver. Under the system procedure, the tablet or token must be slotted into an electric interlocking device at the other end of a single-track section before another train is allowed to pass. The tablets were discs made of metal or fibre, with a gunmetal weight at the top of the magazine, engraved with the names of the stations between which it was valid. Each tablet also had notches to ensure that it would fit only one pair of instruments. The system needed each station at the end of each section to be staffed. The staff member at one would communicate with the staff member at the other end of the section with a bell code to release a tablet. With advances in electrical locking of lever frames within signal boxes, the tablet instrument also electrically locked the section signal lever. Accordingly, that was marked with a white stripe on the red background.

Tyer's tablet system came in different sizes and models. Widespread in the UK was Tyer's No. 6 tablet instrument, which had a cast-iron frame with a movable drawer at the front, which issued and received the tablets. On the left-hand side was a lever to reseat the tablet when it was replaced into the magazine. It had wooden side cheeks to access the complicated mechanism and a tombstone-shaped wooden case on the top which housed the bell plunger, commutator and the tablet indicators for Up and Down trains. At the very top was the galvanometer. The signalling bell associated with the machine was separate so could be located on the block shelf or wall-mounted above the instrument. The No. 6 instrument was adopted by most railway companies on single-line installations, while the Great Western Railway used Tyer's No. 7 electric train tablet instrument at several locations, including the Bampton to Witney section of line.

Born in Kennington on February 6, 1830, Edward Tyer was educated first at the City of London School and afterwards privately. After spending a short period in his uncle's City office, he decided to turn his attention to the development of electrical appliances, work for which he had already shown considerable aptitude. In 1852, aged just 22, he took out a patent for an electrical signalling device operating on locomotives. It turned out to be the first of a long series of inventions that would revolutionise railway-signalling systems. His tablet system was introduced in England in 1878 before being adopted by much of the rest of the world. Tyer was also a pioneer in telegraphic communication, as he was the originator of the enterprise, which would later become London's postal telegraph service. He was a Fellow of the Royal Astronomical, Geographical, and Microscopical Societies, a Member of the Institution of Electrical Engineers and an Associate of the Institution of Civil Engineers. He died at Tunbridge Wells on Christmas Day, 1912, aged 83.

It is impossible to calculate how many disasters have been avoided because of Tyer's tablet system, which went a very long way to eradicating the human error responsible for so many of them, especially in the case of Thorpe in 1874. As such, its immense contribution to railway safety cannot be calculated. On the UK national network the use of Tyer's system is now almost extinct, with most lengthy single-track lines having been converted to more modern systems such as Tokenless Block or Radio Electronic Token Block. In 2016, the Tyer Electric Token Block (using No. 7 instruments and coloured Perspex tablets) remained in use on the Stranraer Line, between Girvan and Dunragit. Tyer's system was used in New Zealand for a century up to 1994, and Sri Lanka Railways still use it. Examples of the instruments can be seen on heritage railways, either in use or on display.

Chapter 6

1876 ABBOTS RIPTON: DOUBLE COLLISION ON THE EAST COAST MAIN LINE

An accident on a blizzard-hit section of the East Coast Main Line led to fundamental changes in British railway signalling practice. Abbots Ripton station would be all but forgotten but for a rail disaster with far-reaching consequences. The station, 4½ miles to the north of Huntingdon, which served the small Cambridgeshire village, was opened on November 1, 1885 and closed on September 15, 1958, before anyone in railways had heard of Dr. Beeching. Yet it became the scene of a pivotal moment in British railway history. For it was here that on January 21, 1876, when the Great Northern Railway's southbound 10-coach 'Special Scotch Express' (known as the 'Flying Scotsman' after 1923), running late in a snowstorm and at its top speed of 40-45mph, was involved in a double collision.

The blizzard conditions on the night were directly to blame. The semaphore signal arms had been frozen by heavy snow, and so the signals showed 'clear'. The express driver therefore had no warning of the presence of a coal train backing on to the main line from a siding, and so a collision was inevitable. Minutes afterwards, a northbound express from London to Leeds hit the wreckage. In all, 13 people died, leaving 53 passengers and six crew members injured. Up to then, the Great Northern's section of the East Coast Main Line had a safety record second to none, and was considered to be exemplary for railway safety. That record disappeared in a few horrendous moments.

THE FIRST COLLISION

The 'Scotch Express' that evening included among its passengers the Russian ambassador, the deputy chairman of the GNR and another director, as well as a director of the North Eastern Railway. Also on board was Thomas Elliott Harrison, chief engineer of the NER and a past president of the Institute of Civil Engineers. That afternoon a very bad snowstorm had hit the area surrounding Peterborough and Huntingdon, with snow and sleet freezing as it fell on to already cold ground and equipment. The southbound coal train had left Peterborough about 18 minutes late, and therefore with about 12 minutes less lead on the 'Scotch Express' than normal. Running in front of the 'Express' it was scheduled to be shunted into a siding at Abbots Ripton to allow the faster train to pass.

The snowstorm had delayed both trains and so the signalman at Holme, the station north of Abbots Ripton, decided to direct the coal train into sidings there to allow the 'Express' to pass, to avoid being delayed by the coal train, and set his signals accordingly. The signalman urged the driver to hurry up, as he was, "keeping the Scotchman standing at Wood Walton (the previous signal box)." However, the coal train ignored the signals, or could not see them, when it arrived at Holme at 6.21pm. It did not stop and carried on past Holme towards Abbots Ripton where the shunting movement originally took place.

The Holme signalman telegraphed Abbots Ripton 'box that the train had run past the signals, and told the station master at Holme that the train had disobeyed the signals. Meanwhile, the 'Scotch Express' had left Peterborough at 6.24pm, six minutes late, and 'did not slow down to take into account the bad weather. The express passed through Holme at about 6.37pm, the signals all showing clear, and arrived at Wood Walton at 6.40pm. The signalman there had set his signal levers to danger to protect the shunting at Abbots Ripton, but had not left his levers to set detonators at the home signal, nor did he supplement his fixed signals by displaying a hand-lamp from the signal box. He told the subsequent inquiry he was busy stopping a train of empty coal wagons on the Down line; because of the weather he did not hear the express until it ran past his cabin at full speed. At 6.44pm the 'Scotch Express' reached Abbots Ripton, its driver having seen, "nothing but white lights all the way from Peterborough." Travelling at the full speed of 40-45mph, it crashed into the coal train, which had not yet cleared the main line after almost completing the scheduled shunting movements.

Several wagons were smashed, but the coal train locomotive escaped serious damage, while the express engine derailed, veered to the right and ended up lying on its side, leaving its tender and two carriages blocking the Down line. The 'Scotch Express' guards walked back up the Up line towards Wood Walton, laying detonators on the rails to warn any further trains to stop. Despite the signals showing all clear, the Manchester express stopped in response to the Wood Walton signalman using a handlamp to show a red light from his signal box. It finally pulled up beyond the Wood Walton Down distant signal. From there, the Abbots Ripton Up distant signal could be seen ahead showing the clear white all-clear. The Manchester express then moved cautiously towards Abbots Ripton, being stopped successively by the 'Scotch Express' guard waving a red handlamp and then by a platelayer, eventually drawing up at the rear of the wrecked passenger train.

The railway also used lower quadrant semaphore signals to work the block system. A lever in the signal box was connected by a wire (under tension, and passing over intermediate pulleys) to a counterweighted arm on the signal. To set a signal to all clear, the signalman pulled the appropriate lever in his signal box; this moved the arm down (which was pivoted in a slot in the signal post), against the pull of the counterweight, 'to a vertical position in the post.' When the lever was moved to set the signal to danger, this did not positively drive the signal to 'danger' but paid out slack in the wire and allowed the counterweight to take the arm to a horizontal position. Since by day the signal arms were clearly visible from the signal box from which they were worked, the system had no repeater in the 'box to confirm a signal was actually showing the aspect corresponding to the lever position.

In emergencies, the signal could be set to danger by cutting the wire; but a heavy weight lying on the wire would keep the signal at all clear by effectively pulling on it. Since the signals were normally set to all clear, any fault stopping them from being moved would almost certainly keep them at 'all clear' as well. At night, or in poor daytime visibility, an oil lamp displayed a white light when the signal was at 'all clear'; when the signal arm moved to the horizontal 'danger' position it brought a red lens in front of the light, so that a red light was then displayed to oncoming trains.

In poor visibility, GNR regulations called for detonators to be laid, if possible, on the track at the home signal when this was set to danger. At stations where platelayers were available, this should also be done at the distant signals. In this case, however, it was found that the weight of snow on the semaphore arm, and snow and ice on the wires by which the arm was moved, prevented the signals from showing danger, after signalmen had pulled the levers. While this would not have been so great a problem on a clear day, in snowstorms, signalmen could not see the signals. Accordingly, the 'Express' passed a series of signals, which had been set to danger, but were showing clear. Therefore, it may be considered as an accident waiting to happen.

THE SECOND COLLISION

The coal train engine was still functional and ran light to Huntingdon to seek assistance. Dazed by the events, the Abbots Ripton signalman set his signals in both directions to danger but did not follow the correct procedure and immediately send the five-beat obstruction danger bell signal to Stukeley, the next signal box south. Instead he tried to send a message reporting the crash and seeking assistance by the speaking telegraph to Huntingdon station. He prefixed the message with the special SP code indicating top priority but the signalman at Huntingdon did not answer. The Abbots Ripton signalman kept trying to raise Huntingdon, but without success and when the Huntingdon signalman did answer he first refused to accept any message not starting with a code to indicate time sent, and rebuffed subsequent sends with coded to say he was busy. He certainly was – he was handling the passage of a 13-coach express train running in the opposite direction to Leeds and passing it on to the next signal box.

At 6.52pm, after trying in vain for eight minutes to pass his message to Huntingdon South, the Abbots Ripton signalman at last sent the obstruction danger bell signal to Stukeley. The Down Leeds express passed through Huntingdon at 6.49pm, at which time no message had been accepted there from Abbots Ripton, and reached Stukeley at 6.52pm. The signalman at Stukeley received the obstruction danger message just seconds after the express had passed. The Abbots Ripton Down distant signal was showing 'all clear' and the Leeds express approached it at full speed. The Leeds express ploughed through the tender and carriages blocking the line. It was then that most, if not all, of the deaths were believed to have occurred. Messages seeking assistance were then sent to Huntingdon and Peterborough. It was found that the original cause of the crash was placing far too much reliance on signals and block working that allowed high-speed running – even when the conditions were not suitable. The GNR was using the block system, which everyone believed would prevent such accidents. Accordingly, the details of the accident greatly alarmed other railway companies that relied on it.

Abbots Ripton and Holme had signal boxes and between them were two intermediate boxes. All of them controlled home signals near the box and distant signals about half a mile before the home signals. The line was thus divided into three blocks, each roughly two miles long; entry to each block was controlled by the signal box at the start of the block. Shunting into the siding at Abbots Ripton took place in a fourth block. The home signals at Abbots Ripton were interlocked with the siding points so that whenever the points were open to the main line the Abbots Ripton home signal lever had to be at danger. All signal boxes could communicate with adjacent ones via their block telegraph. Signals were normally kept at all clear but were set to danger to protect trains as follows; when a train entered a block by passing a home signal, the signalman would set the home signal to danger, therefore preventing a following train entering the same block. The distant one would also be set to danger. Trains were required to stop at a home signal at danger but were allowed to pass a distant signal at danger, merely warning the driver of an approaching train to moderate his speed so that the train could be stopped at the home signal. Both signals would be returned to 'all clear' when the next box telegraphed line clear.

SIGNALLING PRACTICES CHANGED FOREVER

A Court of Inquiry, which was held from January 24 to February 17, reported on February 23, and rejected the conclusion of the coroner's jury that the block system was at fault and had proved ineffective in a case of emergency. The problem instead lay with signals, it was said. The court criticised the Holme station master for not stopping the 'Express', the Wood Walton signalman for not using detonators or a handlamp to stop the same train and the delay of the signalman at Huntingdon in answering Abbots Ripton. The inquiry report recommended that signals were improved so that they worked correctly in frost and snow, and that they gave an indication to the signalman if they were not operating properly. Also, it recommended that signals should not normally be set at clear, as had been the standard practice up to then, but at danger, so that if they stuck in bad weather, they would not wrongly show clear. Another recommendation was the use by signalmen of handlamps in bad weather to confirm the indications of fixed signals and the provision of telegraph apparatus in all signal boxes.

The second collision was deemed to have been caused by the inadequate braking performance of the second express and its crew's failure to implement emergency procedures promptly and correctly. Noting that the Leeds express did not have continuous braking, the inquiry also called for improvement of braking systems on trains. It also called for the suspension of less-important trains, and the reduction in speed of other trains, in very severe weather conditions. The express trains were made up of non-bogie non-corridor four- or six-wheeled carriages. There were 13 on the Leeds express, giving a weight (including the engine and tender) of more than 200 tons. At this period, other railways often had to resort to using more than one engine to maintain a high speed, but the Great Northern had one of the best engine classes of the period – the Stirling Singles with their 8ft driving wheels, and so this was not necessary. However, like all other railways, the GNR had considerable difficulties in stopping the trains rapidly once they were at speed.

To stop a train, the driver could shut off steam, get his fireman to apply a handbrake on the tender and send the engine into reverse. He had no means of applying brakes to the rest of the train; indeed, most of the carriages had no brakes. Two or three of the carriages were brake carriages with handbrakes, each with a guard who would apply them if and when he heard the driver 'whistle for brakes'. In trials carried out after the accident under favourable conditions, this method was shown to bring the train to rest within 800-1,150 yards when travelling at 40-45mph. Railway inspectors considered that much shorter stopping distances would be possible if passenger trains were provided with continuous brakes operable by the driver, and had urged such systems be fitted. The railway companies had resisted this as unnecessary, unreliable, expensive and dangerous. Now the GNR was reaping the cost of that decision.

Following an inquiry into the accident, major basic changes in British railway signalling practice were made. The Great Northern had been operating on the block system, which was intended to eradicate such accidents, so the accident caused great concern among railway companies everywhere. The subsequent inquiry into the accident rejected the earlier conclusion of the coroner's jury that the block system was at fault. The problem was that the signalmen could not see the signals they were controlling in the blizzard, and had they done so, they would have seen that they were fixed in position by the weight of the snow and ice. As a result, the modern practice of the default position for signals being 'danger' was adopted. 'All clear' was indicated by a green light, so that a broken red lens no longer gave false reassurance. The Great Northern furthermore adopted a significantly different design of semaphore signal in the form of the 'somersault' signal. The pivot about which the arm moved was at the middle of the arm, so that snow could not significantly affect it. Furthermore, railway companies were required by law to make an annual return to the Board of Trade on what percentage of their coaching stock was fitted with continuous brakes. Eventually, but only after further accidents, continuous braking was fitted to passenger trains

Chapter 7

1879 TAY BRIDGE: THE RAILWAY
TITANIC

When it was opened, Scotland's Tay Bridge was hailed throughout the world as an engineering marvel. Yet within months, it had become immortalised as a byword for railway disasters, after part of it collapsed, taking a train and 75 people on board to the bottom of the river below.

By the middle of the 1860s, the North British Railway was running main line trains to Berwick, Carlisle, Glasgow and Aberdeen. The latter was achieved via the Edinburgh & Northern Railway, later the Edinburgh, Perth & Dundee Railway, which ran from Burntisland on the northern shore of the Firth of Forth. It operated services between Burntisland, on the northern shore, and Tayport, from where a boat took passengers to Broughty Ferry for onwards travel to Dundee and Aberdeen. When it began operating on February 3, 1850, the ferry from Burntisland to Granton was the world's first railway ferry. The Edinburgh, Perth & Dundee Railway became part of the North British on July 29, 1862.

Needless to say, the Aberdeen route was an awkward and finicky affair, which might have been acceptable in the early days of passenger railways, but not at a time when better technology was available. The route involved two crossings of major river estuaries, those of the Forth and the Tay. Passengers were taken across both by ferries, and the final 28 miles into Aberdeen were achieved only with the aid of running rights over the Caledonian Railway's line from Kinnaber Junction. The North British route was the shorter, but far less convenient than the Caledonian Railway counterpart from Edinburgh to Aberdeen, which went around the heads of both estuaries. There was only one long-term solution for the North British; ditch the ferries, and instead bridge the Tay and the Forth. Easier said than done.

Engineer Thomas Bouch had already built an outstanding reputation. He helped develop the caisson, a watertight structure for use in bridge pier building and ship repairs, and also the roll-on roll-off train ferry. For the North British Railway, he designed parts of Edinburgh Waverley station, and also built bridges on the North Eastern Railway's Stainmore route across the Pennines. He first approached the Edinburgh & Northern Railway in 1854 about bridging the Tay, but the money was not available. However, a decade later he was working on plans to cross both the Tay and the Forth. In 1869, the Tay Bridge scheme was revived as a separate undertaking. The North British invested heavily in it, despite public fears that, firstly, a two-mile crossing of the sea could not be built and secondly, if it was, it would not last. The company's shareholders, however, backed it fully, and Bouch was appointed designer and overseer for the project.

The North British Railway (Tay Bridge) Act received Royal Assent on July 15, 1870 with the foundation stone laid on July 22, 1871. Bouch drew up a lattice-grid design, combining cast and wrought iron. The design was well known, having been used first by Kennard in the Crumlin Viaduct in South Wales in 1858, following the innovative use of cast iron in the Crystal Palace. However, the Crystal Palace was not as heavily loaded as a railway bridge. A previous cast-iron design, the Dee Bridge, which collapsed in 1847, failed because of poor use of cast-iron girders.

Bouch's bridge was to be supported by brick piers resting on bedrock, shown by trial borings to lie at no great depth under the river. At either end of the bridge, the bridge girders were deck trusses, the tops of which were level with the pier tops, with the single-track railway running on top. However, in the centre section of the bridge (the 'high girders'), the bridge girders ran as through trusses above the pier tops (with the railway inside them) in order to give the required clearance to allow passage of ships sailing to Perth. However, the bedrock actually lay much deeper than Bouch had ascertained, and he had to redesign the bridge, with fewer piers and correspondingly longer span girders. The new pier foundations were constructed by sinking brick-lined wrought-iron caissons on to the riverbed, and filling these with concrete. To reduce the weight these had to support, Bouch used open-lattice iron skeleton piers, each pier having multiple cast-iron columns taking the weight of the bridging girders, with wrought-iron horizontal braces and diagonal tie-bars linking the columns of the pier to give rigidity and stability. The basic concept was a standard practice of the time, but with the Tay Bridge, the pier dimensions were constrained by the caisson.

Hopkin Gilkes and Co. of Middlesbrough, which had previously worked with Bouch on iron viaducts, and of which his brother was a director, built the bridge. The firm was in financial difficulty and began liquidation proceedings in May 1879, before the disaster. Bouch's brother died in January 1876, and Bouch not only inherited £35,000 worth of Gilkes' shares but also a guarantee of £100,000 of Gilkes' borrowings, leaving him facing potential financial ruin when the firm collapsed in 1880. The change in design of the bridge increased costs and caused delays in its completion. Matters were made worse when two of the high girders fell when being lifted into place during a gale in February 1877. The finished bridge consisted of 85 spans and at the time was the longest in the world. The spans carried a single rail track; 72 of these were supported on spanning girders below the level of the track while the remaining 13 navigation spans were spanning girders above the track.

The first locomotive crossed the bridge on September 26, 1877, carrying local VIPs and senior railway officials. A Board of Trade inspection was conducted over three days of good weather in February 1878 and the bridge was passed for use by passenger traffic subject to a 25mph speed limit. Yet in his report the inspector wrote: "When again visiting the spot I should wish, if possible, to have an opportunity of observing the effects of high wind when a train of carriages is running over the bridge..." Prescient words indeed.

The first fare-paying passengers were carried over the bridge on June 1, 1878. At one mile and 1,705 yards long, the 88ft-tall structure was the longest railway bridge in the world. Its completion was an enormous boost for the North British, which afterwards attracted 84% of the Edinburgh to Dundee traffic, and the bridge was celebrated as a marvel of its age, attracting rich and famous visitors from far and wide. Queen Victoria crossed it in 1879 and knighted Bouch – who, around the same time, began designing a second bridge, this time crossing the Forth at Queensferry.

THE SHORT LIFE OF THE LONGEST BRIDGE
On December 28, 1879, the east coast of Scotland was battered by a Beaufort force 10/11 gale, blowing almost at right angles to the bridge. Described as a hurricane, one local said it was as bad as a storm he had seen in the China Sea. At both Aberdeen and Glasgow, the wind speed was measured at 71mph, and later estimates placed it at 80mph. The line over

the bridge was limited to one train at a time by a signalling block system using a baton as a token. At 7.13pm, a six-coach train from the south slowed to pick up the baton from the signal cabin at the south end of the bridge, then headed out on to the bridge, picking up speed. The signalman turned away to log this and then tended the cabin fire, but a friend present in the cabin kept watching the train.

At a point about 200 yards from the signal cabin, sparks were seen flying from the wheels on the east side, before the train moved into the high girders. The witness then saw, "a sudden bright flash of light, and in an instant there was total darkness, the tail lamps of the train, the sparks and the flash of light all... disappearing at the same instant." A sudden blast shook the cabin. When the train did not appear off the bridge on the line to Dundee, the signalman tried in vain to contact the signal cabin on the north side. All communication with it had been lost, as the block instruments were dead. The bridge had taken the full force of strong side winds and the central section, the 'high girders', had collapsed, taking the train with it. A sailor on board the training ship *Mars*, which only a few months before had fired a salute as Queen Victoria's Royal Train had crossed the bridge, saw the lights of the train then heard the blast. He saw a gap in the bridge, and no sign of the train.

At first it was hoped that the train had reached the opposite bank, but the truth began to dawn, firstly when mailbags were washed ashore and then when a fisherman found a carriage ventilator and a Dundee and Burntisland destination board in the sea at Tayport. Daylight broke to show that the entire section of high girders from pier 28 to pier 41 had vanished. All passengers on board, some of them having travelled from King's Cross, died. It was estimated that 74 or 75 people lost their lives, but nobody has ever established the exact number. Only 46 of the bodies were ever found, while some were never identified. The approximate number of victims was established by painstaking examination of ticket sales. Fifty-six tickets for Dundee had been collected from passengers on the train before crossing the bridge, but season ticket holders, tickets for other destinations, and railway employees would have added to that figure. Divers exploring the wreckage later found the train in the river still within the high girders, with the engine inside the fifth span of the southern five-span division.

BADLY DESIGNED, BADLY BUILT AND BADLY MAINTAINED

The disaster sent shock waves both through the country and the Victorian civil engineering sector. A Court of Inquiry was established in a bid to establish the reason for the collapse. The court heard that the masonry of the pier bases showed poor adhesion between stone and cement, while the hold-down bolts to which the column bases were fastened were poorly designed, and burst through the masonry too easily. On the southernmost fallen pier, every tie-bar to the base of one of the columns had had a packing piece fitted. Bouch said that while 20psf (design pressure, pounds per square foot) had been discussed, he had been guided by experts to assume 10psf and therefore made no special allowance for wind loading. After hearing expert evidence of defects in workmanship and design detail, it found that, "the fall of the bridge was occasioned by the insufficiency of the cross bracing and its fastenings to sustain the force of the gale." The court said that if the piers, and in particular the wind bracing, had been properly constructed and maintained, the bridge could have withstood the storm that night, albeit with reduced safety levels.

Bouch's choice of cast iron as a building material was seriously questioned. Painters who had worked on the bridge in the summer of 1879 said that it shook when a train went over it, and the shaking got worse when trains went faster. While the North British

Railway maintained the tracks, Bouch was retained to supervise maintenance of the bridge. He had appointed Henry Noble, a bricklayer, not an engineer, as his bridge inspector, as he had worked for him on the construction of the bridge. While checking the pier foundations to see if the riverbed was being scoured from around them, Noble had become aware that some diagonal tie-bars were 'chattering', and in October 1878 had begun rectifying this. At the hearing, Bouch's counsel attempted to suggest derailment of the train and collision with the girders were the true cause, but expert witnesses roundly demolished such claims. However, there were strong suspicions that shoddy workmanship at the Wormit Foundry, where the iron girders were manufactured, may have been equally responsible if not more so. The inquiry concluded that the bridge was, "badly designed, badly built and badly maintained." It said: "The fall of the bridge was occasioned by the insufficiency of the cross bracing and its fastenings to sustain the force of the gale."

Bouch's reputation lay in unredeemable tatters. He was mainly blamed for the collapse in not making sufficient allowance for wind loading. There was also evidence that the central structure had been deteriorating for several months before the disaster, with indications that joints had loosened. In his book *Red for Danger*, transport historian and pioneer Talyllyn Railway preservationist Tom Rolt wrote: "The sensation caused by the fall of the bridge has no parallel in railway annals and is comparable only with that occasioned by the loss of the *Titanic* many years later." Bouch's hopes of being allowed to rebuild the Tay Bridge were understandably dashed. The Board of Trade set up a commission to consider what wind loading should be assumed when designing railway bridges. It recommended that structures should be designed to withstand a wind loading of 56psf.

A new steel Tay Bridge was built by the North British Railway, 59ft upstream of the original, under the direction of William Henry Barlow, who had engineered the Midland Railway's London extension and designed its London terminus at St Pancras. He also helped complete Isambard Kingdom Brunel's Clifton Suspension Bridge four years after the Great Western Railway engineer died. Barlow sat on the commission that investigated the causes of the Tay Bridge disaster and designed the replacement, with his son Crawford Barlow as engineer. The new design used large monocoque piers to support a double-track railway. The brick and masonry piers from the first bridge were kept as breakwaters for the new piers upstream. William Arrol & Company of Glasgow built the new bridge, with work starting on July 6, 1883 and the bridge opening on July 13, 1887.

Bouch had also been engineer for the North British, Arbroath & Montrose Railway, which included an iron viaduct over the South Esk. Examined closely after the Tay Bridge collapse, the viaduct as built did not match the design, and many of the piers were noticeably out of the perpendicular. After vigorous tests with stationary and rolling loads over a 36-hour period, the structure was seriously distorted and pronounced unsafe. Bouch's Redheugh Bridge, a road crossing on the Tyne at Newcastle, was built in 1871 but was condemned in 1896. The structural engineer who condemned it said that the bridge would have blown over if it had ever experienced wind loadings of 19psf. Bouch died a few months after the public inquiry into the Tay Bridge disaster ended, his health having severely deteriorated.

The locomotive that had collapsed into the Tay, 1871-built North British 4-4-0 No. 224, was later lifted out of the river estuary, only to be dropped again. However, it was eventually recovered, rebuilt and returned to service, remaining in use until 1919. Nicknamed 'The Diver', several superstitious drivers refused to take it over the replacement bridge. The disaster remains one of the world's most famous bridge failures and is still one of the worst structural engineering failures in the British Isles. Historians still debate about the actual cause, and whether Bouch was blamed to a greater extent than he should have been.

BRITAIN'S FIRST ALL-STEEL BRIDGE

Regardless of the disaster, the North British had seen only too well the immense value of bridging the 'unbridgeable' and pressed on with plans to build a second bridge to shorten the route to Aberdeen. Bouch had proposed a suspension bridge across the Forth and his scheme reached the point where the foundation stone was laid. However, the inquiry's findings that his Tay Bridge had been under strength stopped the project. As a direct result, the design of the Forth railway bridge was quickly transferred to Sir Benjamin Baker and Sir John Fowler. Fowler and Baker came up with a cantilever design; the first bridge in Britain to be constructed entirely from steel. It was built by Arrol & Co, between 1883-90. However, during its construction, more than 450 of the estimated 4,600 workers were injured and 98 lost their lives... a death toll exceeding that of the Tay Bridge disaster. Nonetheless, the Forth railway bridge was, and still is, regarded as one of the greatest engineering achievements in the history of civilisation.

Stretching 1.6 miles from North to South Queensferry, the main crossing comprises tubular struts and lattice girder ties in double cantilevers, each connected by 345ft 'suspended' girder spans resting on the cantilever ends. It has two 1,710ft main spans of 521.3m, two side spans of 680ft and 15 approach spans each 168ft long. Standing 151ft above high tide and weighing 50,513 tons, it used nearly 65,000 tons of steel, 18,122cu m of granite and 6.5 million rivets. At the busiest time, 4,600 men and boys worked on the bridge, a boy throwing the glowing rivets to each three-man team. Where possible, natural features were incorporated into the design for added stability, such as the island of Inchgarvie, and the headlands and high banks on either side. The double-track bridge was officially completed on March 4, 1890 when the Prince of Wales, the future Edward VII, tapped an inscribed golden rivet into position. The bridge cost £3,227,000 to build, nearer to £235 million by today's standards.

Bettering the routes to Aberdeen offered by the Caledonian, it provided a huge boost to the fortunes of the North British, but it was not owned outright by that company. A conference at York in 1881 had set up the Forth Bridge Railway Committee, to which the North British agreed to meet 35% of the cost. The Midland Railway agreed to contribute 30%, while the rest came equally from the North Eastern Railway and the Great Northern Railway. As with the East Coast Joint Stock, it was yet another example of the very close co-operation that led to the eventual unification of services on the ECML. On October 16, 1939, the first Luftwaffe attack on Britain in the Second World War took place over the Forth Bridge, when Nazi bombers attacked the Royal Navy base at Rosyth. The incident also saw the first German planes to be shot down over Britain during the conflict, thanks to the RAF's 603 (City of Edinburgh) Spitfire squadron. A 14-year restoration completed in 2011 at a cost of £130,000,000, included painting it with 250,000 litres of glass-flake epoxy resin as used on North Sea oil rigs, expected to last at least 20 years.

INSPIRATION FOR A 'POOR' POET

Scottish weaver, poet and actor William Topaz McGonagall (March 1825-1902) is best remembered for his poem, *The Tay Bridge Disaster*, and also because he was widely considered to be an extremely bad poet. He wrote about 200 poems, and despite the damning criticism of many of them, collections of his verse remain popular, with volumes available today. He was parodied by, among many others, the *Monty Python's Flying*

Circus team, who in one episode created a Scottish poet called Ewan McTeagle, whose poems were no more than requests for money in non-rhyming prose. As *The Tay Bridge Disaster* concerns visionary ideals that plunged into total disaster, it mirrored his own career.

THE TAY BRIDGE DISASTER
by William Topaz McGonagall

Beautiful Railway Bridge of the Silv'ry Tay!
Alas! I am very sorry to say
That ninety lives have been taken away
On the last Sabbath day of 1879,
Which will be remember'd for a very long time.
'Twas about seven o'clock at night,
And the wind it blew with all its might,
And the rain came pouring down,
And the dark clouds seem'd to frown,
And the Demon of the air seem'd to say-
"I'll blow down the Bridge of Tay."
When the train left Edinburgh
The passengers' hearts were light and felt no sorrow,
But Boreas blew a terrific gale,
Which made their hearts for to quail,
And many of the passengers with fear did say-
"I hope God will send us safe across the Bridge of Tay."
But when the train came near to Wormit Bay,
Boreas he did loud and angry bray,
And shook the central girders of the Bridge of Tay
On the last Sabbath day of 1879,
Which will be remember'd for a very long time.
So the train sped on with all its might,
And Bonnie Dundee soon hove in sight,
And the passengers' hearts felt light,
Thinking they would enjoy themselves on the New Year,
With their friends at home they lov'd most dear,
And wish them all a happy New Year.
So the train mov'd slowly along the Bridge of Tay,
Until it was about midway,
Then the central girders with a crash gave way,
And down went the train and passengers into the Tay!
The Storm Fiend did loudly bray,
Because ninety lives had been taken away,
On the last Sabbath day of 1879,
Which will be remember'd for a very long time.
As soon as the catastrophe came to be known
The alarm from mouth to mouth was blown,
And the cry rang out all o'er the town,
Good Heavens! The Tay Bridge is blown down,

And a passenger train from Edinburgh,
Which fill'd all the peoples' hearts with sorrow,
And made them for to turn pale,
Because none of the passengers were sav'd to tell the tale
How the disaster happen'd on the last Sabbath day of 1879,
Which will be remember'd for a very long time.
It must have been an awful sight,
To witness in the dusky moonlight,
While the Storm Fiend did laugh, and angry did bray,
Along the Railway Bridge of the Silv'ry Tay,
Oh! Ill-fated Bridge of the Silv'ry Tay,
I must now conclude my lay
By telling the world fearlessly without the least dismay,
That your central girders would not have given way,
At least many sensible men do say,
Had they been supported on each side with buttresses,
At least many sensible men confesses,
For the stronger we our houses do build,
The less chance we have of being killed.

Chapter 8

1887 HEXTHORPE: THE WORST DAY
AT THE RACES

A crash involving three trains at Hexthorpe, near Doncaster, on September 16, 1887, left 26 people dead and raised big questions over the effectiveness of simple vacuum braking systems. The St Leger Stakes, a flat horse race run at Doncaster, was established in 1776 and is the oldest of Britain's five Classics. It is the last of the five to be run each year, and its distance is longer than any of the other four. It has also long been hugely popular as a day trip destination, and after the railway arrived, many specials were laid on to bring visitors to each event. Hexthorpe railway platform lies 1½ miles to the west of Doncaster on the line between the town and Sheffield and Barnsley. It was then a simple wooden structure normally used for the collection of tickets from the trains arriving for the St Leger meeting. The usual method of working this section of line was to pass trains from Hexthorpe Junction under a 'permissive' block ruling, not usually used on passenger lines, with additional control by two flagmen spaced between the junction box and the ticket platform. The platform was situated within a block section between Hexthorpe Junction and Cherry Tree Lane and so had no signals of its own.

On Friday, September 16, 1887, two trains were in the section. The first, a Midland Railway train, stood at the platform, the second, a Midland Railway special race excursion train, was waiting just to its rear. As the first train moved off, the second moved on to the platform so that tickets could be checked. As the race train was standing at the platform for the tickets to be collected, a Manchester, Sheffield & Lincolnshire Railway train from Manchester to Hull, the driver of which had over-run danger signals, crashed into the rear of the stationary train. The driver and fireman of the MS&LR train were uninjured but 25 people were killed in the Midland train, the last three coaches of which, all third class, were smashed to pieces. The chimney of the MS&LR locomotive was broken off and the buffers damaged. The sound of steam escaping from the engine was mixed with the screams of the injured and dying. Chaos ensued as people tried to escape the carriages and, within an hour, 50 people had been removed from the train and were being treated on the platform by doctors and surgeons from neighbouring towns. It was decided that most of the injured should be sent to Doncaster Infirmary and carriages were soon being used to transport the more seriously injured.

Within four hours, 23 bodies had been recovered from the wreckage – an arduous task as, owing to the nature of the accident, the bodies were packed tightly together and had to be removed with saws and hatchets, it was reported. Walter Middleton, a Sheffield cabman, who was doing, as hundreds of other cabmen from local towns had been doing – taking people from Doncaster station up to the course during the St Leger week – went to Hexthorpe directly he heard of the accident... and found his wife Elizabeth and their year-old infant among the dead. Mr and Mrs J. Beaumont, of the Theatre Tavern, Arundel Street, Sheffield, were both killed, leaving a family of five orphans, the youngest only 13 months old. John Goldsmith, landlord of the Royal Oak in Cemetery Road, Sheffield, had a compound fracture of one leg and a simple fracture of the other and was taken to Doncaster Infirmary with the rest of the injured. He remained in hospital until December 15 when he was moved back home, accompanied by a police inspector and two constables. He seemed to be on the mend, but took a turn for the worse, however, and on March 6, 1888, he died at home as a direct result of his injuries, taking the number of fatalities to 26.

THE LORD CHIEF JUSTICE DELIVERS HIS VERDICT

The Monday after the accident, Major Marindin, of the Board of Trade Railway Inspectorate, visited the site and then went to the Doncaster offices of the MS&LR where it was proposed to hold the inquiry. However, demand for space from those wishing to attend was such that it took place in the room where the local board of guardians held its meetings. Mr Warren, a solicitor from Leeds, represented Samuel Taylor, the driver of the MS&LR train, and had also been engaged to watch the proceedings on behalf of the local branch of the Amalgamated Society of Railway Servants, a forerunner of today's Rail, Maritime & Transport Union. Mr Holmshaw, district superintendent of the MS&LR, stated at the opening that although the block system of signalling had been in use on the line since 1880, it was always suspended on St Leger and Cup race days. Notice was given to all drivers to proceed with caution, to be on the lookout for flag signals, and to have their trains well under control. Similarly, special instructions were issued to signalmen not to lower their signals until they were satisfied that the speed of approaching trains had been reduced. Flag signalmen on the ground had instructions to keep red flags displayed until the ticket platform had been cleared.

The Hexthorpe Junction signalman, Thomas Welham, who had served in that 'box for 30 years, said that when the second train approached, his distant signal was at danger and the ground signalmen were showing red flags. He gave a caution signal (in those days a green flag – white was for 'all clear') to the driver of the MS&LR train as it passed his 'box. Two of the ground signalmen, George Coates and Joseph Frost, said that they waved their red flags to warn the approaching train. John Mason, the driver, and Patrick Mitchell, the fireman of the Midland train, said their train had first stopped before reaching the ticket platform to allow a train already there to clear it; when this happened they drew their train forward into the platform and stopped again for the tickets to be examined. Samuel Taylor, the driver of the MS&LR train, said that he was under the impression that he would not have to stop at Hexthorpe, as he thought the tickets had been collected at Conisborough. On approaching Hexthorpe Junction, before the ticket platform, he noted that both distant and home signals were at danger. He shut off steam between them and subsequently the home signal was cleared. His train was then travelling at about 14mph and he did not see any caution signal from Hexthorpe Junction signal box. On passing the junction his mate saw an advance signal and called out: "Right, mate!" On looking he saw that it was off. He saw no train ahead until he got on to straight track when it was about 200 yards away; his train was then travelling at about 35mph. He applied the vacuum brake (Smith simple system), opened the whistle and put his engine in reverse, while his fireman opened all the sand valves. He said that he struck the stationary train at about 10mph. He had seen no red flag signals, though his fireman claimed, after the collision, that he had seen them.

Employees of the MS&LR (which later became the Great Central Railway) offered to give up a day's wages to help pay for the cost of the accident. However, the directors declined, saying they did not consider it consistent with their duty to tax to such an extent those who lived by the sweat of their brow. The *Penny Illustrated Paper* expressed the hope that the Board of Trade would instruct railway managers in future to cause the block system to be strictly acted upon, not only on ordinary occasions but on extraordinary ones as well. At the resumed inquest, the chairman of the MS&LR, Sir Edward Watkin, expressed his sympathy and said that he and his fellow directors did not dispute their liability and offered to deal quickly and satisfactorily with claims. The trial of the MS&LR driver and fireman at York, before the Lord Chief Justice, was the first big legal case in which the newly formed trade union ASLEF took part and for which it engaged eminent counsel to defend its members.

The jury returned a verdict of not guilty with the Lord Chief Justice making damning comments about braking systems. He said in his summing up that, "...he could not but think that the railway company was seriously to blame for having had in use a brake which not only was not the best in existence, but which was known to be insufficient and liable to break down." The management were "thick skinned" over all safety matters and in this case Sir Edward Watkin, the company chairman, said, "...it was a misfortune that the Lord Chief Justice should have exonerated the driver and fireman." However, the Hexthorpe accident, closely followed by the Armagh rail disaster in Northern Ireland as described in the next chapter, marked the beginning of the end of the 'simple' vacuum brake.

Chapter 9

1889 ARMAGH: NO BRAKING THE RUNAWAY TRAIN

The fourth-worst British railway disaster in terms of fatalities occurred on June 12, 1889 when 80 people were killed in what became known as The Runaway Train crash, prompting the government to push through pivotal legislation making continuous brakes, locking of facing points and block signalling mandatory. That fateful Wednesday, at Armagh on the Newry and Armagh section of the Great Northern Railway (Ireland), a special excursion had been laid on for 800 people – 600 of them children on an Armagh Methodist Church Sunday school outing – to travel from Armagh to Warrenpoint. However, 941 people turned up to board the train at Armagh; the Sunday school outing marching there accompanied by the band of the 3rd Battalion of the Royal Irish Fusiliers. The heavy demand meant that the train had to be lengthened from 13 to 15 vehicles. Yet that load was clearly far too much for the rostered engine, Beyer, Peacock main line express passenger 2-4-0 No. 86, with 6ft coupled wheels, which was unsuitable for the three-mile climb, much of it 1-in-75.

The irate driver, Thomas McGrath, who had only travelled on the branch as a fireman before, refused to take the train, because he said that No. 86 was not fit for purpose. However, he was eventually overruled, persuaded, cajoled or taunted, by the Armagh station master, into taking the regulator. To prevent people without tickets joining the excursion, once each compartment had been checked its doors were locked. Two hundred yards from the summit, his train stalled. The Dundalk superintendent's chief clerk, James Elliott, was on board and directed the train crew to divide the train and proceed with the front five coaches to Hamiltonsbawn station, about two miles away, and leave that portion there, before returning for the second portion. Owing to limited siding capacity at Hamiltonsbawn, only the front five vehicles could be taken on to there; so the rearmost 10 vehicles would have to be left standing on the running line. Yet once this rear portion was uncoupled from the front one, the continuous brakes on it would be released, and the only brakes holding it against the gradient would be the hand-operated brakes in the rear brake van. Improvised braking took the form of stones placed behind nine of the rear portion's wheels. However, as No. 86 prepared to steam off with the front portion, it set back about a foot and the resultant buffering-up was enough to overcome that minimal braking effect.

To everyone's horror, the rear 10 coaches began to run back down the steep gradient and gather speed back towards Armagh station. Despite frantic attempts to recouple the two halves of the train while the coaches were still moving slowly, they accelerated down the bank, reaching a speed of 40mph with many of the passengers trapped in locked compartments. The line was operated on the time interval system, rather than block working, so there was no means at Armagh of knowing that the line was not clear. The required 20-minute interval before letting a fast train follow a slow one had elapsed, and the next scheduled passenger train had left Armagh. Its lead locomotive, Sharp, Stewart 0-4-2 No. 9, was slogging up the gradient with the 10.35am Armagh to Newry service when the runaway coaches, which had by then reached a speed of up to 40mph, smashed into it with devastating consequences. No. 9's driver saw the runaway train coming and braked to 5mph, but was helpless to stop any collision. His fireman leapt to safety, and the driver stayed on the footplate to the last, escaping unscathed.

The three rear carriages all but disappeared, as did their trapped occupants. The two rearmost vehicles of the excursion train were utterly destroyed, and the third severely damaged. The debris tumbled down a 45ft embankment. The impact threw No. 9 on to its side with the connection to its tender lost. This train was also fitted with 'simple' (non-automatic) continuous vacuum brakes, and these were lost when the engine became disconnected. The train split into two sections, both running back down the gradient towards Armagh. Application of the handbrakes on the tender and on the brake van by crew members brought the front and rear halves of the scheduled train to a stop without further incident. Out of the passengers in the excursion, 80, many of them children, died and 260 were injured. It was the worst rail disaster in the UK in the 19th century, and remains Ireland's worst-ever railway disaster.

The immediate cause of the tragedy was the lack of the application of sufficient brake power to hold the rear nine coaches and brake van of the excursion train. It is believed that the disaster could have been prevented if the excursion train been fitted with an automatic continuous brake as opposed to only a non-automatic continuous brake. There were, however, stories of heroism on the darkest day in Irish transport history. A Sergeant Woodward of the Royal Highland Fusiliers saw that a collision was imminent and leapt out of a carriage door on to the footboard. He grabbed hold of four children and dropped them to safety, and then leapt for his own life. He then returned to the crash site to help remove the dead and wounded from the wreckage. As part of his investigations, the Board of Trade inspector criticised the allocation of an engine with only just enough power to haul a 15-coach train over the Armagh bank, although he accepted that it could be done.

Two witnesses had seen the brake working properly before the train left Armagh; the brake apparatus had been found in the wreckage and appeared to be in good working order. However, the rear portion that ran away had done so with the braked wheels revolving freely. Therefore, either the guard had not applied the brake properly, or passengers in the brake carriage had tampered with it. The blame was laid mainly at the door of Mr Elliott, who had ordered a course of action that ignored company rules and stipulated that the main guard should not leave his van until perfectly satisfied that his brake would hold the train. Furthermore, the more junior guard should have gone back down the track to protect the train. The locomotive shed foreman at Dundalk was criticised for not sending a more experienced driver and choosing an engine that was borderline adequate for the purpose.

The report criticised the over-confidence of the driver of No. 86 as to the capabilities of his engine and regretted that his better judgment in at first refusing to drive it must have been overcome by the words of the Armagh station master. The inspector said that passengers should not have been allowed to travel in brake vans and called for the practice to be banned. He said that the train should not have been as big, and been limited to 10 vehicles, and that carriage doors should not have been locked. The inquest into the disaster finished on June 21, 1889, and made findings of culpable negligence against six of those involved; those at Dundalk responsible for selection of the engine, the driver and both guards on the train, and Mr Elliott, who had taken charge. As a result, three of the accused were committed for trial for manslaughter. Elliott was tried in Dublin that August, but the jury could not agree on a verdict, and so a retrial was ordered. That took place in October, and he was acquitted. The cases against the other two defendants were then dropped. The railway had suspended Elliott after the accident and he was later sacked. After he was acquitted, he was presented with £65, what had been left over from £117 collected by GNR(I) railwaymen to pay for his defence, highlighting the fact that he was a popular figure. He took a new job as chief clerk in a Dundalk firm of hardware merchants, and died on June 9, 1938, aged 86.

Patrick Murphy, the driver of No. 9, escaped injury in the crash but was unable to return to work. A month after the disaster, the GNR(I) gave him £300 in compensation, but he died on January 5 the following year. Questions to president of the Board of Trade, Sir Michael Hicks Beach, revealed that in the whole of Ireland, only one locomotive and six vehicles were equipped with an automatic continuous brake, in England 18% of the passenger rolling stock had no continuous brake, and a further 22% had non-automatic brakes; in Scotland 40% of the passenger rolling stock was without continuous brakes. The British public was outraged, and within two months of the Armagh disaster, Parliament was forced to rush through legislation in the form of the Regulation of the Railways Act 1889, enforcing critical safety measures that are still part and parcel of our national network today. They included the absolute block system and the mandatory fitting of continuous automatic brakes, requests for which from the Board of Trade had all but fallen on deaf ears for many years.

This legislation is widely considered as the end of the Victorian tradition of government non-interference in private railway company business and the beginning of the modern era in UK rail safety. Rarely has a railway accident had more resounding repercussions. A commissioned sculpture of a little girl carrying a bucket and spade commemorating those who died in the disaster was unveiled in The Mall in Armagh on June 12, 2014. Northern Ireland regional development minister, Danny Kennedy, unveiled the statue as part of a series of events taking place to mark the 125th anniversary of the disaster. He said: "The great tragedy of the Armagh railway disaster led directly to various safety measures becoming legal requirements for railways in the United Kingdom, and encouraged a move towards direct state intervention in such matters." Days earlier, Armagh Methodist Church held two special services at Abbey Street. An opening service was conducted by former Methodist president, the Rev. Ken Todd, and the closing service featured a school choir and the Armagh Old Boys Band.

—————————————— *Chapter 10* ——————————————

1890, 1939, 1978 NORTON FITZWARREN: SOMERSET'S TRIPLE ACCIDENT BLACKSPOT

The Somerset village of Norton Fitzwarren, where the GWR Minehead branch, now the West Somerset Railway, leaves the West of England main line, has been the scene of three major disasters. When the broad gauge Bristol & Exeter Railway opened through Norton Fitzwarren on May 1, 1843, the nearest station was two miles to the east at Taunton. The original West Somerset Railway was opened to Watchet on March 31, 1862, leaving the main line at Norton Junction, but still no station there was provided. The first section of the Devon & Somerset Railway to Wiveliscombe opened on June 8, 1871, connecting to the West Somerset line just west of its link with the Exeter line, turning Norton Fitzwarren into a busy junction. At long last, a two-platform station was opened on June 1, 1873, located immediately east of the junction.

A relatively quiet station, albeit on a busy main line. However, that all changed when at 12.36am on November 11, 1890, a Down goods train from Bristol to Exeter, hauled by both a standard-gauge engine and a broad-gauge pilot engine, (as by then this section of line had become mixed gauge) arrived at Norton Fitzwarren to both take on and detach stock. Another Down goods train, which was not scheduled to stop at Norton Fitzwarren, was due at 1.17am. At 1.05am, the signalman told the guard of the first goods train to shunt it clear of the Down line, on to the Up main, while the pilot engine was separately moved on to a branch line. After the fast goods train had passed, the signalman moved the pilot engine back to the Down main line, and while this movement was taking place, at 1.23am, the Up special boat train from Plymouth to Paddington was offered to the signalman by the preceding signal box. It was GWR practice that upon the arrival of steamers at Plymouth, a special mail train with letters and passengers to London and beyond would be despatched. Such a working had departed from Plymouth with around 50 passengers on board after a steamship from the Cape of Good Hope had landed mail and passengers.

Forgetting that the slow goods train was still on the Up main line, the signalman accepted the 'Cape Mail' boat train, and duly cleared his signals for it. At 1.24am, the boat train, which comprised two eight-wheeled composite coaches and a van headed by an 0-4-0 saddle tank, passed the signal box at 50mph, and ran into the goods train. The driver and fireman of the goods train managed to jump clear before the accident, but were unable to give any signal in the short time they had. The guard of the boat train later said that he was not aware of any braking before the impact. Ten passengers were killed, and 11 people (including the driver and fireman of the boat train) were seriously injured. The boat train footplate crew would have been killed but for the fact that their engine had behind it a heavy coal tender, which telescoped into the front carriages, and bore the brunt of the crash. Flames from the locomotive set fire to the smashed front coach, which, like others of the day, was of wooden construction. Six of the occupants burned to death. Most of the dead and injured were miners returning to the north of England from the South African goldmines. Some of them possessed considerable sums in gold; one had

£90-worth – a fortune in those days – on his body. Both locomotives were completely wrecked, the broken carriages and debris being piled to a height of 13ft. In one carriage the occupants, including a woman and several children, had a miraculous escape, the glass in the windows of theirs not even being broken, while every other compartment was smashed. It took several hours to free all the passengers from the train.

The accident was primarily down to the fact that signalman George Rice had forgotten that the goods train was still on the main line after being shunted, and allowed the boat train into his section with the line obstructed. However, the Board of Trade inquiry inspector, Colonel Rich, ruled that a contributory factor was the premature change of the goods train's headlamp from red to green; it may have been the case that the driver of the boat train would have noticed a red lamp ahead of him in time to apply his brakes, especially as it was a clear night. Another contributory factor was the failure of the guard of the goods train to notify the signalman of the presence of his train on the main line, as required by the rules of the company. Rice, who had worked on the railway for 35 years, had a spotless record. However, several months before the crash, he was knocked over by a pilot engine while crossing a line, and although he recovered, had reportedly since then appeared at times unwell, although he was deemed quite capable for duty. By his own admission, he had felt "bad in the head" the whole evening before the crash. The coroner's jury at the subsequent inquest returned a verdict of manslaughter against him.

However, the findings of the inquiry made a significant contribution to rail safety. Colonel Rich was told during his investigations that signalmen had a practice of inserting a flag stick in the spring catch of a signal lever of a blocked line to stop them forgetting that a train is waiting. The colonel's suggestion that a "mechanical contrivance marked train waiting" should be fixed to leves in signal boxes to do the same job, and to stop the levers being pulled in error, was widely taken up. Lever collars and clips became standard practice across the network. Furthermore, following the inquest, 12 refuge sidings for slow trains were built by the GWR between Exeter and Weston-super-Mare.

DERAILMENT OF THE NIGHT SLEEPER

In 1931, the GWR embarked on a project to quadruple the track between Cogload Junction, where the main line from Bristol Temple Meads and the North met the Castle Cary cut-off line from Yeovil, Reading and Paddington, for the seven miles south through Taunton to Norton Fitzwarren. There, the existing station buildings were demolished, to allow a new Up-relief line to be built north of the existing northern platform, followed by the creation of a Down relief road south of the southern platform. A new metal passenger bridge was erected, connecting the new station buildings to the north with both island platforms. The completion of the project on December 2 that year also allowed the GWR to create the large regional goods facility at Fairwater Yard, located just east of the station.

By World War Two, Taunton had become a major railway junction, situated on five miles of quadruple track, which stretched from Cogload Junction to the Down end of Norton Fitzwarren station. Railway operations during the blackout were particularly difficult and late running was very common, even if no bombs were falling near the tracks. On November 4, 1940, the 13-coach 9.50pm sleeper train for Penzance with around 900 passengers on board, headed by GWR 4-6-0 No. 6028 *King George VI*, was running 68 minutes late when it called at Taunton. Hard on its heels was a lightly loaded newspaper train from Paddington heading to Penzance, and it was decided to give this priority over the sleeper. The latter was accordingly signalled to remain on the Down relief when it left the main Down platform at Taunton, instead of being switched to the

Down fast on its right. Great Western locomotives were driven from the right-hand side of the footplate. Although the majority of the company's very distinctive lower-quadrant signals were on the left of the track they controlled, their siting took account of this.

In this case, however, the driver, P.W. Stacey, wrongly assumed that he had been rerouted back to the Down main line when leaving the station, and the signals were showing clear for another train coming from behind on the adjacent track. The sleeper driver continued to misread the signals thereafter until the newspaper train suddenly overtook him on his right, and then he realised his mistake… by which time disaster was only some 300 yards ahead. The driver of the sleeper train left Taunton station and observed the indications of the right-hand signals (all green, indicating 'proceed' for the Down main line), not realising his train was travelling on the Down Relief (left-hand) track. Wartime blackout conditions at night contributed to this misapprehension.

The signals had been badly placed as an economy measure. If at least one pair of signals had been placed as usual – requiring a gantry or a bracket – then the driver of the train would have been more likely to recognise which track he was on and which signals related to it. The signals at Norton Fitzwarren were fitted with the GWR Automatic Train Control, which alerted the driver in the cab, audibly, that the approaching distant signal was at 'caution'. A warning signal had to be acknowledged or the brakes would be applied. Unfortunately, drivers could be so used to cancelling the warning, that they may have done this subconsciously.

This would especially happen if the driver was reading the wrong green signal. Although the ATC equipment was working correctly, wartime deferred maintenance had meant that in a number of cases the ATC ramps were not working correctly and were giving false 'caution' alerts when the signals were clear, supposedly a correct failure mode, but one that to crews believing that a warning when they saw clear signals was just another maintenance issue. Indeed, it appeared that the sleeper driver must also have cancelled an ATC warning, but, with the end of the four-track section coming up, there was no time to stop the train before it reached the open catch-points at the country end of Norton Fitzwarren station. The driver realised his mistake only when the newspaper train overtook the sleeper, by which time it was too late to stop. The 'King' class locomotive sped through the catch-points and finished up in a field, the leading six coaches piling up behind, and spreading wreckage across the other tracks. The crash occurred at a point on the railway where four tracks were reduced to two.

The guard in the end vehicle of the overtaking train was alarmed by strange noises, which later turned out to be ballast thrown up by the derailing train alongside. He applied his own brakes to check what might be the problem, and the train stopped at Victory Siding, the next signal box to the west. He discovered the sides of the last vehicles were scored from flying ballast, and that there were broken windows. The derailing 'King' locomotive had nosed down off the end of the overrun siding and then swung across the main tracks, only feet behind the overtaking train. Twenty-seven passengers and the fireman on the sleeper, W. Seabridge, were killed, and 75 injured, 56 seriously enough to need hospital treatment. Thirteen of the dead were naval personnel and 16 of the injured were also in the services. The first ambulance arrived at 4.30am after the station master raised the alarm, and 10 ambulancemen from the GWR's staff assisted with just handlamps and torches illuminating the crash site. Breakdown gangs arrived from Taunton, Newton Abbot and Swindon from 6.20am onwards. The Up main line was reopened for traffic shortly after 8pm the same day and the Down main line the following evening. The ATC apparatus on *King George VI*, which survived largely intact because it had fallen into soft ground, was found to be working perfectly. The locomotive was subsequently repaired and returned to service.

In concluding his report into the accident, Ministry of Transport inspector Lieutenant-Colonel Sir Alan Mount said: "The accident was not due to enemy action or to sabotage; nor were the permanent way, works, or signalling equipment concerned in any way. The sole cause was an unaccountable lapse on the part of driver P.W. Stacey, who is an experienced and capable man in the top link at Old Oak Common Shed, with an excellent record and 40 years' service. He mistook the line on which he was running, and, while disregarding the relief line signals, he was observing those for the main line, which were all clear for the newspaper train. He frankly admitted his responsibility, but his account of what happened, given in good faith, appears to have been affected by his experiences. I am forced to this conclusion that his memory of the circumstances which led to his initial mistake on starting from Taunton was, in fact, unreliable, and that his error must have been the outcome of failure to concentrate." Mention was also made in the report that Stacey's house in Acton had been hit by a bombing raid that morning. Regardless of the damage, he had reported for work as usual on the day of the crash. While the inspector spoke with sympathy about the driver, the accident was blamed on his human error rather than absence of failure of warning apparatus, not relevant in this case. In more recent times, a number of comparably situated sets of catch-points such as those at Norton Fitzwarren were removed from the UK network.

DIRTY BED LINEN LEFT 12 DEAD

The third major disaster near Norton Fitzwarren also involved a sleeping car train. However, this time it had nothing to do with movements on the track, a driver's error or missed signals, but by sacks of dirty bed linen which had been placed in front of an electric heater. The fatal fire started in British Railways Mk.1 sleeping car No. W2437 in the early hours of July 6, 1978.The vehicle was built in 1960, at which time trains in the UK were still mainly hauled by steam locomotives, which provided steam for heating passenger accommodation. However, first generation diesel locomotives of the period were fitted with boilers so that they could be used with existing coaches. However, with steam locomotives gone by the 1970s, and with boilers proving unreliable and expensive to maintain, the decision was made to change to electric train heating, and W2437 was converted in 1976, with an electric heater being installed in the vestibule.

The Class 47-hauled 10.30pm sleeping car express from Penzance to Paddington was scheduled to pick up two sleeping cars at Plymouth, so that passengers joining the train there could go to bed without having to wait for the main service to arrive at around midnight. The main store for bed linen on the Plymouth service was at Old Oak Common depot near Paddington. Used bedding from Plymouth was previously transported in the guard's van of the Plymouth portion, but in 1977 that vehicle was removed from the formation of the sleeper train. Instead, the dirty linen was stacked in plastic bags in the vestibule of W2437… against the heater. The train arrived at Plymouth from Penzance at 11.50pm. It was coupled up to the Plymouth sleeping cars (which included W2437) and the electric heating was switched on at 15 minutes past midnight. The train departed on time at 12.30am and made scheduled stops at Newton Abbot and Exeter – while, unknown to anyone else, the bags of linen were heating up.

They began to smoulder and give off toxic gases, including carbon monoxide. Worse still, the carriage ventilation system drew fresh air from the vestibule, and the gases were sucked into the system and into each berth. Fire broke out and began ripping through the vehicle. An attendant pulled the communication cord, and the train was stopped at

2.41pm near Silk Mill signal box, a mile before Taunton. By that time, most of the 12 victims were already dead from carbon monoxide poisoning. The sleeping car attendant of the Plymouth coaches could only shout a warning to a few of the occupants before he was overcome by smoke. Several passengers woke up and were able to escape, although they had considerable difficulty in doing so due to the smoke and heat. Initial reports showed that fire crews, who arrived on the scene within four minutes, had difficulty in rescuing passengers because doors on the train were locked. That practice was against BR rules, but it was commonplace for attendants to lock the end doors of the pair of coaches that they were responsible for, as it helped to keep out intruders. British Rail's chief operating manager William Bradshaw confirmed that it was company policy to lock doors connecting carriages, but not external doors while the train was in motion. Several MPs called for external doors to remain unlocked. Local residents from Fairwater Close in Taunton went to help survivors from the train and provided tea, blankets and comfort in their homes. Injured passengers were taken to the nearby Musgrove Park Hospital for treatment.

LOCKED DOORS "NOT TO BLAME"

Five days later, the inquest at the coroners' court in Taunton found that nine of the deaths were caused by asphyxiation, one by a heart attack and one by heart failure and smoke inhalation. Most of the bodies were found in the sleeping compartments. While 11 died on the train, a 12th passenger, a Belgian national, died from pneumonia the following month, having never regained consciousness. All of the dead or injured were in the front two carriages of the 12-coach train. In February 1980, the final report into the blaze was published by inspector Major Tony King. It stated the cause of the accident as burning linen stacked too close to a heater. It also suggested better training of carriage attendants and better safety features. The investigation found that although some of the train doors were locked, this was not the main cause of death. As a result, British Rail made it clear that all doors were to be left unlocked at all times. The Taunton fire occurred just as new Mk.3 sleeping cars were at the design stage. The decision was taken to install state-of-the-art fire prevention measures including sophisticated warning systems, fire retardant materials, multilingual warning placards and revised emergency procedures. Mk.1 sleeping cars were phased out of main line service by the early 1980s.

Chapter 11

1896 PRESTON: AN END TO SPEED

A derailment at speed by an express train at Preston station in Lancashire in 1896 miraculously left just one fatality. However, the repercussions were enormous. Overnight the accident forced a sea change in public opinion against trains travelling at excessive speed, and effectively stalled major developments in that department until the 1930s.

The train in question was hauled by LNWR locomotives No. 2159 *Shark* and No. 275 *Vulcan*, which were easily capable of handling the 200-ton load, but neither driver had driven this particular train before. Furthermore, neither had experience of driving a train non-stop through Preston. A sharp curve at the north end of the station by the goods yard meant that there was a 10mph restriction. In an instant, the entire train was ploughing its way along the permanent way, but, thanks to the presence of mind of the drivers and despite the weight and vast momentum of the train, it was brought to a standstill within a distance of 80 yards. Although the engines and the leading coaches were badly damaged, the train stood the tremendous strain remarkably well. As it happened, it was lightly loaded and only one of its 16 passengers, a young man called Donald Mavor, was killed. However, despite the very low casualty count, the accident sent shockwaves through the rail industry that would hamper progress for the next four decades. It was later ascertained by Board of Trade accident investigator, Colonel York, that the express had been travelling around 40-45mph through the station.

When it hit the speed-restricted curve, instead of going around it the train effectively carried on in a straight line. The engines ploughed through the goods yard, with the train coming to rest just short of a bridge wall. Both engines remained upright but the carriages were scattered across the mangled tracks and one of their occupants was fatally injured. At the Park Hotel, Preston, the town coroner opened an inquest on the body of Donald Mavor, with Mr J. Fenner, solicitor to the company, Mr J. Shaw, superintendent, and Mr Price, district superintendent, present. At the outset Mr Fenner, on behalf of the company, expressed the sorrow, which he said it felt that such an accident should have occurred on its line.

The subsequent Board of Trade inquiry at Preston heard Colonel York conclude: "The cause of the accident is clear. A reverse curve without any intervening tangent, without a check rail, with super elevation suitable only for very low speeds, badly distributed and with a radius at one point of only seven chains; a train drawn by two engines, each having a rigid wheelbase of 15ft 8in; and lastly a speed of 40mph or more form a combination of circumstances which were almost certain to lead to disaster." Without wanting to sound facetious, just one fatality in a train of the period might sound hardly worth the headlines given the death toll of the Tay Bridge or Armagh disasters. Yet the repercussions were resounding. Overnight, public opinion towards 'speeding' trains changed for the worse. There was outright hostility to what was widely seen as placing life and limb at risk for the sake of breaking speed records in pursuit of railway company prestige.

THE RACES TO THE NORTH
The Preston accident effectively ended the period known as the 'Races to the North' in

49

which the operators of the East and West Coast Main Line routes competed against each other to offer the shortest distance between London and Glasgow. By late Victorian times, train travel had long been an accepted part of everyday life, and it was no longer a novelty to complete a journey that previously took several days by road in just a few hours. Emphasis shifted to how quickly that journey could be undertaken. It may seem incredible today, in this age of health and safety first, but for two summers in the late 19th century, companies on the rival routes agreed to race public passenger-carrying trains.

In late 1887, the East Coast companies decided to allow third-class travel on their 'Special Scotch Express'. In response, in May 1888, the LNWR and Caledonian announced without prior warning that from June 2 they would speed up the 10am 'Day Scotch Express' and run it from Euston to Edinburgh in nine hours, the time taken by the East Coast alternative from King's Cross. A fortnight later, the East Coast responded by increasing the speed of its services from July 1, 1888. While the West Coast cut an hour off from its 10-hour journey time, the East Coast reduced its nine-hour journey by 30 minutes. In retaliation, the West Coast companies cut 30 minutes off, before the East Coast again cut off half an hour. The West Coast did likewise. It appeared the rivals had decided to run their trains as fast as the technology of the day would permit. The East Coast had a great advantage as it utilised one of the most famous class of 'singles', those designed by Patrick Stirling for the Great Northern.

At first, the rivals attempted to keep the 'races' secret, but the press soon picked up on them. There were fears that passengers might be deterred from riding on fast trains; it was within living memory that some declined to ride through tunnels or over high viaducts. Those who had been on board the racing trains might well have been blissfully ignorant of the fact. However, by the mid-1880s, it was also clear that large numbers of passengers welcomed faster trains as opposed to cheaper fares, especially on the Anglo-Scottish routes. On Bank Holiday Monday, August 8, 1888, the West Coast decided to match the East Coast's eight-hour schedule. It kept up this fierce competition for a week. The East Coast partners then announced that from August 14, the journey would be cut to 7hrs 45mins, with the fastest train taking 7hrs 27min. Responding, the LNWR and Caledonian ran from London to Edinburgh in 7hrs 38mins on August 13, with an average speed of 52.3mph. The following day, the rivals reached agreement on minimum timings for their trains, and racing stopped. However, to get the last word in, on August 31, a King's Cross-Edinburgh train ran as fast as possible, recording an average speed of 52.7mph. That September, the races were well and truly over, with both sides having gone back to the July timetables, the East Coast railways taking 8hrs 15mins and the West Coast 8hrs and 30 minutes. The rivalry erupted again with the imminent completion of the Forth Bridge, which would give the Eastern partners a shorter route to Dundee and Aberdeen.

The second Race to the North, a term used by transport historians to describe these two periods of intense competition, came in the summer of 1895, and involved night expresses running between London and Aberdeen. The 'finishing post' was Kinnaber Junction, 38 miles south of Aberdeen, where the Caledonian Railway and the North British Railway routes joined before running into the Granite City over Caledonian metals. The two routes ran either side of Montrose Basin on the approach to the junction, and journalists covering the races could see their trains racing against each other. One such race saw both trains reach Kinnaber Junction at the same time. The Caledonian signalman sportingly decided to let the rival North British Railway train through, and it reached Aberdeen in 8hrs 40mins from King's Cross, compared with

the standard 12hrs 20mins before the races began. The following night, the West
Coast responded by making an 'exhibition run' from Euston via Crewe to Aberdeen in
8hrs 32mins.

On August 20, the Great Northern Railway's Stirling Single 4-2-2 No. 668 took the
East Coast express 105.5 miles from King's Cross to Grantham in 1hr 41mins with an
average speed of 62.7mph. The overall 393-mile trip was covered in 6hrs 19mins, at a
speed of 63.5 mph, while the extended run to Aberdeen, making a total of 523 miles, took
8hrs 40mins, with an average speed of 60.4mph. The LNWR responded two days later,
with Improved Precedent express passenger 2-4-0 No. 790 *Hardwicke* taking 2hrs and
6mins to cover the 141 miles from Crewe to Carlisle, reaching 88mph in places, with
an average speed of 67.1mph, setting a new speed record in the Races to the North. The
Improved Precedents were designed by Francis Webb and built at Crewe Works, 166 in
batches between 1887-97, and two more in 1898 and 1901. They were among the most
famous British steam locomotives of the 19th century. They were not only capable of
high speeds but regularly hauled heavy loads in relation to their small size, hence their
nickname 'Jumbo'.

Even more famous than *Hardwicke* was No. 955 *Charles Dickens*, which hauled the
8.30am express from Manchester to Euston and the 4pm return for 20 years. In doing so
it clocked up more than two million miles, a record that has never been broken by any
other British steam locomotive. Yet again, steam was shrinking the world. In the wake
of the 1895 races, overall train speeds of some express services had notably increased to
bring down journey times. In June 1896, the rivals negotiated a minimum journey time
for the Anglo-Scottish trains to reduce the possibility of danger at excessive speeds, but
the agreement applied only to daytime services, not those that ran at night. The express
that came to grief at Preston was scheduled to maintain an average speed of 60mph for
105 miles of its journey, relying especially at night on pinpointed enginemanship.

NOT ONLY BUT ALSO
Before the Preston incident, two other serious accidents, this time on the East Coast
route, had served to heighten public concerns over express rail travel. Both involved
Stirling Singles, the stars of the Races to the North. The first, 40 yards south of St Neots
station on November 10, 1895, saw No. 1006 hauling the night 'Scotch Express' from
King's Cross when a rail broke as the engine passed over at 60mph. The train was
derailed, scraping along the platform leaving a trail of debris, and parted company with
the coupling of the second sleeping car. Four out of nine coaches at the rear of the train
became separated from the train formation and crashed into loaded coal wagons in a
siding to the north of the station. The front part of the train came to a standstill about
a quarter of a mile further on. There was one death, a Miss Louisa O'Hara, who was
thrown out of the sleeping car and struck her head against a goods wagon. Six passengers
were severely injured, the guard also having struck his head.

On inspection the fractured faces of the broken rail were clean and bright, so it was
clear that no inspection could have previously found a fault. The railway company
blamed faulty manufacture, suggesting the cast iron was too brittle. Sir Francis Marindin
of HM Railway Inspectorate suggested that the first fracture of the rail took place at a
tiny flaw over a chair, which did not exist when it was manufactured. He also commented
on the abnormally heavy axle loading of the locomotive, with nearly 20 tons on the
driving axle. The second incident, also involving trackwork, this time at Little Bytham on
Stoke Bank on March 9, 1896, saw an Up 'Leeds Diner' hauled by No. 1003 at 70mph
at a section where not only had ballasting not been completed, but the flagman whose

job it was to provide warning of a speed restriction had been removed prematurely. The unballasted track became distorted by the engine movement and several carriages at the rear became detached, one hitting a bridge parapet and dividing from its underframe, killing two passengers, with another coach running down the embankment into a field. Following the accident, the weight of this locomotive was reduced to reduce the risk of broken rails.

DON'T MENTION THE 'S' WORD

Denbighshire West MP Herbert Roberts raised the case of the Preston accident in the House of Commons days later. He said: "I beg to ask the President of the Board of Trade whether his attention has been called to the serious accident which occurred to what is known as the London and North Western 'Racer' at Preston... on its journey from Euston to Aberdeen, a train which held the record this year for travelling 105 miles in 105 minutes; and whether, in view of the great risks to the travelling public connected with this practice of rival railway companies racing to Scotland, the Board of Trade will make strong representations to the said companies on the subject?" However, the President of the Board of Trade declined to officially ban high-speed trains. He said: "I am not prepared to admit that high speed means danger."

Yet Britain's railway companies nonetheless sat up and took notice of the growing public concerns over excessive speed. The bad publicity that followed in the wake of the Preston crash was seen as having changed public opinion, and safety concerns rather than speed were paramount once more. An agreement of limiting speed was reached between the two rivals, and lasted until 1932. Also, it was realised that the racing trains had greatly inconvenienced passengers because instead of arriving at Aberdeen at around 7am as scheduled, they reached their destination in the early hours of the morning, leaving them to wait on a deserted station platform for onward travel.

Such was the public fear of trains running at too high a speed that when the Great Western Railway's No. 3440 *City of Truro* allegedly became the first in the world to break the 100mph barrier, touching 102.3mph with the 'Ocean Mails Special' from Plymouth to Paddington on Wellington Bank in Somerset in May 1904, the company kept quiet about it for many years. A report of the 100mph record appeared in a newspaper the following day, after a mail van worker on board conducted some unofficial timings of his own, but the report by and large went unnoticed by the rest of the world's media. Charles Rous-Marten, who recorded the speed on board the footplate of the locomotive, at first restricted his reporting of the speed achieved on the day to just the minimum of 62mph logged on the ascent of Whiteball summit. In *The Railway Magazine*, he merely described the trip as setting "the record of records", adding: "It is not desirable at present to publish the actual maximum rate that was reached on this memorable occasion." Yet it was only in the December 1907 edition of *The Railway Magazine* nearly four years later that the alleged speed appeared to a wider public for the first time, and even then was not attributed to a particular engine. Although the GWR and its rival, the LSWR, were locked in a race for the ocean mails traffic, neither had any intention of admitting actions that might appear reckless. At the time, the GWR allowed only the overall timings for the run to be published. Readers had to wait until the following April's edition for its identity to be revealed.

City of Truro's legendary but unofficial record came nearly five years after a series of high-speed test runs took place on the Lancashire & Yorkshire Railway's Liverpool Exchange-Southport line using locomotives from Aspinall's newly introduced 'High Flyer' 4-4-2 class. On July 15, 1899 one such train was formed of Southport-based No.

1392 and five coaches. Timed to leave Liverpool Exchange at 2.51pm, it was allegedly recorded as passing milepost 17 in 12.75mins. That gave a start-to-pass speed of 80mph but, given the permanent 20mph restriction at Bank Hall and the 65mph restriction at Waterloo, the suggestion has been made that this train attained 100mph. The L&Y never published details or timings of this test run. It is only because local enthusiasts 'unofficially' noted the passing times that this obscure 100mph claim is known at all.

In his volume *The Lancashire & Yorkshire Railway* (Ian Allan, 1956), researcher Eric Mason wrote: "It is likely that the event will probably be regarded in the same light as the GW *City of Truro* run, because it is alleged no proper records were kept, it has in recent years been taken, rightly or wrongly, with a large pinch of salt." Another of the 4-4-2 class, No. 1417, became enshrouded in 'mythical legends' over its performances. Mason wrote. "Whilst there is no confirmation of an alleged 117mph near Kirkby, there is no doubt whatsoever that the engine did perform some really fast running in the capable hands of driver J. Chapman of Newton Heath."

After the Preston disaster, the old East and West Coast rivalries were suppressed for several decades although they never went away. An LNWR apprentice under Francis Webb at the time of the Races to the North was young Herbert Nigel Gresley, who went on to become the Chief Mechanical Engineer of the LNER and, it is argued by many, the world's greatest steam locomotive designer.

BEFORE WE WERE SO RUDELY INTERRUPTED...
The 1896 Preston derailment hit a wrong note with public opinion at the wrong time, and led to a cessation of speed record attempts for the best part of the next three decades. However, by the time that the LNER and rival LMS were ready to take up the baton again, lessons had been learned and the network was a safer place. An official record of a steam locomotive breaking the 100mph barrier would not be claimed until November 30, 1934, when Gresley's LNER A3 Pacific No. 4472 *Flying Scotsman* achieved the feat travelling between Leeds and King's Cross. Four years later, the LNER established an all-time world record for steam locomotive speed, when A4 streamlined Pacific No. 4468 *Mallard* reached 126mph during a descent of Stoke Bank in Lincolnshire on July 4, 1938.

The Thirties were the zenith of the steam age, the great decade when, before the clouds of war appeared on the horizon, the steam locomotive concept was taken to dizzy new heights that back in Victorian times few would have imagined possible. Speed record after record was broken as the East and West Coast line operators tore up their 1896 agreement to stop racing, and once again, it was the sky's the limit on the great run from London to Scotland. On the West Coast, the LMS had Swindon-trained Chief Mechanical Engineer William Stanier – who would go on to be knighted in 1943. Facing him was the East Coast's Nigel Gresley. The competition between the pair to produce the best and most powerful locomotives pushed the transport technology of the day to its utmost limits and a few miles beyond. Most importantly, Britain – the country that had invented the steam locomotive – was left standing head and shoulders above the rest of the world in terms of transport. Yes, in the three decades since Preston, priceless safety lessons regarding running express trains at speed had been learned and implemented. However, as *Flying Scotsman* and *Mallard* set the world ablaze with their feats, it had become a distant memory.

Chapter 12

1896 SNOWDON: FATALITY ON
THE FIRST DAY

B ritain's heritage railways have an exemplary safety record, and have long been an integral part of the nation's tourist economy. However, a runaway train with fatal consequences marred the opening day of the Snowdon Mountain Railway, Britain's only rack-and-pinion line, on Monday, April 6, 1896.

The idea of building a Swiss-style railway to the summit of Snowdon, the highest peak in England and Wales, was first proposed in 1869, when Llanberis became linked to Caernarfon by a branch of the LNWR. In 1871 a Bill went before Parliament, applying for powers of compulsory purchase for a railway to the summit, but local landowner, Mr Assheton-Smith of the Vaynol Estate, thought that a railway would spoil the scenery, and so he opposed it. However, nothing happened until 1893 when the Rhyd Ddu terminus of the North Wales Narrow Gauge Railways was renamed Snowdon, attracting many of the tourists who previously visited Llanberis and affecting the livelihoods of the accommodation providers who were Assheton-Smith tenants. After much persuasion, Assheton-Smith ultimately agreed to the construction of a railway to the summit.

By then, no Act of Parliament was required, as the line was built entirely on private land obtained by the mountain railway company, without any need for the power of compulsory purchase. It was designed to the pattern of the rack-and-pinion system patented by the Swiss engineer Dr. Roman Abt facilitating the essential extra adhesion needed for steam locomotives to climb severe gradients. The system uses double-rack rails, fastened to steel sleepers between the running rails. Each locomotive is equipped with toothed cogwheels, which engage the rack and provide all the traction necessary to scale the steepest inclines. On the way down, the rack-and-pinion system also acts as a brake. The railway was laid to the common mountain railway gauge of 2ft 7½in, and runs to a length of four miles 1,188 yards and has an average gradient of 1-in-7.86, while the steepest gradient on the route is 1-in-5.5.

For the line's opening, three 0-4-2 tank engines were ordered from the Swiss Locomotive & Manufacturing Co. of Winterthur. The boilers of the engines were inclined to ensure that the boiler tubes and the firebox remained submerged when on the gradient, the standard practice on mountain railways. The railway was constructed between December 1894, when the first sod was cut by Enid Assheton-Smith (after whom locomotive No. 2 was later named), and February 1896, at a total cost of £63,800. Tracklaying had to start from one end of the line, to ensure the rack was correctly aligned, so although the first locomotives were delivered in July 1895, very little track was laid until August, when two large viaducts between Llanberis and Waterfall were completed. Progress up the mountain was then quite rapid, with the locomotives being used to move materials as required. Despite the exposed location and bad weather, the first train reached the summit in January 1896, and was set for Easter. On the line, the locomotive always runs chimney first up the mountain pushing a single carriage in front of it. For safety reasons, the carriage is not coupled to the locomotive. Colonel Sir Francis Marindin from the Board of Trade made an unofficial inspection of the line on March 27 that year, and after seeing the automatic train brakes in action for the first time, declared himself satisfied, but recommended that the wind speed be monitored and recorded, and trains stopped when the wind was too strong.

TRAIN TUMBLED DOWN THE MOUNTAINSIDE

On April 4, a train was run by the contractor consisting of a locomotive and two coaches. On the final section, the ascending train hit a boulder that had fallen from the side of a cutting and several wheels were derailed. The workmen on the train were able to re-rail the carriage and the train continued. The railway was officially opened two days later, when two trains were despatched to the summit. On the first return trip down the mountain, possibly owing to the weight of the train, locomotive No.1 *Ladas,* driven by William Pickles from Yorkshire, with two carriages, lost the rack a few hundred yards above Clogwyn station. Pickles had great difficulty keeping the engine under control. The wheels jumped the rail, the train thereby losing its ability to brake, and it ran away. Pickles applied the handbrake but it did not work, and with the train now gathering speed downhill he and his fireman leapt off the footplate. *Ladas* continued its descent, going faster every second until, failing to negotiate a left-hand curve, it toppled and fell over the side of the mountain.

Surprised climbers coming up the mountain towards Clogwyn said that they thought they saw a huge boulder falling towards them – but it was the runaway engine tumbling down the mountainside. The two carriages gathered speed until, at last, the automatic brakes slammed on and they came to a graceful halt. One passenger, Ellis Roberts of Llanberis, had seen the footplate crew leap off the engine and decided to follow suit. However, he smashed his head on the rocks and debris alongside the line, suffering a major loss of blood, and died a few days later. In misty weather conditions, the second train, oblivious to the fate of *Ladas*, ploughed into the rear of the carriages at Clogwyn, derailing the engine.

The opening of a railway unique in Britain had attracted many amateur photographers, several of whom rode on the ill-fated train. One of them wrote: "The two trains reached the summit in safety. It was a grand ride, but the weather was foggy. At the top of Snowdon, where it was very cold, we stayed 10 minutes. The return journey began all right, although the 'going' was rather jerky. Suddenly our engine increased its speed to an alarming extent, the cogwheels having got out of gear. Leaving the rails, the engine plunged down the precipice. Fortunately, the brakes prevented our carriages from following it. The cars having stopped, I got out with the rest of our passengers and photographed the scene. Just afterwards the second train came dashing through the dense fog and collided with the other carriages, setting them going again. They came to a standstill a little lower down, and I followed them up in time to take a snapshot of the alarmed passengers leaving the carriages of the second train. Several people were badly hurt. Finally, I took a photograph of the wrecked engine at the bottom of the pass and went home thankful that I had not been toppled over with it."

A subsequent inquiry concluded that the accident had been triggered by post-construction settlement, compounded by excess speed caused by the weight of the train. The line was closed for just over 12 months, with no further trains running until April 9, 1897. As a result of the ensuing inquiry's recommendations, the maximum allowed train weight was reduced to the equivalent of one-and-a-half carriages, leading to lighter carriages being bought and used on two-carriage trains. A gripper system to improve safety was also installed. The line today is a major tourist attraction.

Chapter 13

1906 SALISBURY:ONE FAST CURVE TOO MANY

The 1896 Preston crash as described in Chapter 11 may have, by and large, brought a swift end to racing trains. Yet why then did a boat train in competition with a rival company's service take a 30mph curve at Salisbury station at 70mph, resulting in a crash that left 28 passengers dead?

The Great Western Railway and its great rival, the London & South Western Railway, had long competed to see which could bring the mail from American liners in Plymouth to London in the shortest time. Churchward's 4-4-0 *City of Truro* unofficially broke the 100mph barrier with its 'Ocean Mails Special' in 1904, a fact that the GWR reluctantly admitted only many years later.

At 1.57am on July 1, 1906, an LSWR Saturday boat train from Plymouth Friary to Waterloo carrying 43 first-class passengers failed to navigate a very sharp curve at the eastern end of Salisbury station. The more affluent transatlantic passengers often chose to take the boat train from Plymouth, the first point of landfall in England, to London, thereby gaining a day over those who sailed on to Southampton and Portsmouth and make the journey from there. The curve had a 30mph limit, but the express was travelling in excess of 70mph. The train was completely derailed, and smashed into the London to Yeovil milk train running in the opposite direction and a stationary goods train that was in what is now Platform 6, killing 28 people, including the boat train driver, the fireman of the goods train engine and the guard of the milk train, as well as injuring 11 others.

The three leading vehicles of the express were overturned, going in several directions; the frames stripped of woodwork and completely destroyed. The fourth vehicle fared little better, but comparatively little damage was done to the last vehicle, which came to rest in an upright position with the last pair of wheels on the rails. The locomotive and tender were both overturned on their right sides, but sustained less damage than would be expected, and the engine was shortly afterwards hauled from Salisbury into Nine Elms depot for repairs. Five out of 10 milk wagons were destroyed in the impact. One carriage was said to have run over Fisherton Bridge and the body of a passenger who was flung out was found in shrubbery below.

Salisbury station inspector, John Spicer, reported that the boat train was going much faster than the permitted 30mph. A porter, busy at work on the platforms with the early-morning milk traffic, was visibly shaken by what he saw. He told the *Daily Mirror*: "It is difficult for me to tell you what I did see at first. It was over far quicker than I am able to say the words, and I can only think now of the terrible cries and the awful sights that followed the smash. I was at my work as usual, thinking that it would soon be daylight, when I heard in the distance the rumble of an express. 'That's the American special,' I thought, and stopped for a moment to let her go through. She came up with a little shudder, as I should judge, about 65mph, roaring into the station. Before I had more than caught a glimpse of her, the smash came. I can't describe it. It seemed that there was a great crash first, and then the whole train leapt from the rails and sank down again with a frightful rending, tearing sound." Another witness said: "To my mind the accident was brought about because the boat train was half an hour late in starting from Plymouth. I remember finding the body of the stoker shot right across the platform, close up to the wall. I helped to move that and other bodies."

Bill Abbott, carriage inspector of Salisbury yard, knew how the lighting worked and crawled in, turning off the gas and oil reservoirs to prevent the risk of an outbreak of fire in the wooden-bodied coaches. Doctors were summoned and local people joined in the rescue operation en masse. The ladies' waiting room on Platform 4 became a morgue for a week while other waiting rooms were turned into first aid rooms where medics assessed the injured, many of whom were taken to Salisbury Infirmary. Sydney Chick, the fireman on the stationary goods train, and the driver, Joseph Mortimer, were badly scalded, but both refused medical treatment and stretchers in favour of others and made their own way to the Infirmary. Chick was far more badly scalded than Mortimer, and most of his skin came off with his clothes. He died at 1pm that day.

The *Salisbury Times* reported: "As day dawned on Sunday, Salisbury was the scene of an unparalleled catastrophe." The mayor of Salisbury, Fred Baker, telegrammed the American ambassador expressing Salisbury's regret at the loss of so much American life. US president, Teddy Roosevelt, responded with a letter of thanks to Salisbury Infirmary. The tragedy also made headlines in the *New York Herald* and other US newspapers. The accident occurred at the same time as the GWR was opening a short cut on its West of England Main Line. It was therefore alleged that the driver of the boat train was trying to show that the LSWR was also capable of competitive speeds. Rumours abounded. Some said that rich New Yorkers travelling from the transatlantic port at Plymouth had bribed the driver to run the train as fast as possible, but there was no evidence of this: indeed, the train had lost time earlier. It was stated that drivers often ran through Salisbury very fast on these trains to 'get a run' at the following hill.

The boat train engine was a new LSWR L12 class 4-4-0 with a higher centre of gravity than the earlier T9 'Greyhound' 4-4-0s. At Templecombe, driver William Robins and fireman Arthur Gadd, together with engine No. 421, relieved the crew that had brought the five-coach train from Plymouth, as was the standard practice. It is now believed that the accident was caused, not by racing, but was more likely down to the driver not realising the level of risk that he was taking, especially as this was the first occasion on which he had taken a non-stopping train through Salisbury. Remember – it was not for another half century that steam engines were equipped with speedometers. In presenting his report on the accident to the Board of Trade, Major J.W. Pringle called for the 30mph restriction on the curves at the east end of the station to be cut to 15mph. As a result of the tragedy, all trains were required to stop at Salisbury station from that point onwards, without exception. The speed limit on the curve east of Salisbury was also reduced to 15mph – a limit still effective today. A memorial tablet to the 28 victims is to be found inside Salisbury Cathedral. In 2006, historian Jeremy Moody organised a memorial service at the station.

Chapter 14

1915 QUINTINSHILL: BRITAIN'S
WORST RAIL DISASTER

The worst rail disaster in British history in terms of loss of life occurred on the Caledonian Railway main line at Quintinshill near Gretna Green in Dumfriesshire at 6.50am on May 22, 1915, leaving 226 dead and 246 injured. Sloppy working practices by two signalmen, George Meakin and James Tinsley, were blamed for the multiple collision, which resulted in the worst loss of life in British railway history.

On May 22, 1915, Tinsley was booked to take over at Quintinshill signal box, on the West Coast Main Line near Gretna Green, from Meakin at 6am. The pair, however, had come to a private arrangement that whoever was working the 6am shift could arrive later, taking advantage of a free lift on the early local passenger train from Carlisle to Beattock and avoiding the 1½-mile walk from Gretna. To cover up this very informal arrangement, the train register was not completed by the signalmen in accordance with the rules. So Tinsley arrived at Quintinshill on the local train around 6.30am. As the goods loop was occupied with the 4.50am freight from Carlisle, Meakin shunted the local passenger train on to the Up main line. That in itself was not dangerous, but Meakin failed to take the required safety precautions. He didn't inform the preceding signal box at Kirkpatrick, nor did he place a signal lever collar over the relevant signal lever to stop himself from clearing the signal and allowing another train to proceed from Kirkpatrick. The signalmen's faults were exacerbated by local train fireman George Hutchinson, who failed to remind Meakin that his train was standing on the Up main line and should have checked that a lever collar was in place thus preventing the movement of the relevant signal before returning to his train. A further flagrant breach of the rules was taking place in the Quintinshill signal box, where two brakesmen from the goods train were discussing the progress of World War One with Meakin, and distracting him and Tinsley.

At 6.34am, one of the signalmen gave the 'train out of section' bell to Kirkpatrick for the coal train, which now stood in the Up goods loop. However, neither signalman followed it up with the 'blocking back' signal to Kirkpatrick. Four minutes later, a northbound express from Carlisle passed Quintinshill. At 6.42am, Tinsley was notified about a troop train by Kirkpatrick and accepted it. Four minutes afterwards, he also accepted a second northbound express. At 6.47am he received the 'train entering section' signal from Kirkpatrick for the troop train and offered it forward to Gretna Junction... but completely forgot about the local passenger train on the Up line. When Gretna Junction accepted the troop train, Tinsley pulled his Up home signal to permit the troop train to move forward. If only Tinsley had placed a lever collar on that signal in accordance with stated company practice, and if only fireman Hutchinson had checked, the signal lever could not have been pulled.

At 6.49pm, the 21-vehicle troop train, carrying Territorial soldiers from the 7th Battalion, the Royal Scots, running from Larbert to Liverpool from where they would sail to Gallipoli as part of the 156th Brigade of the 52nd (Lowland) Division, smashed head on into the local passenger train at 6.49am. A minute later, the second express collided with the wreckage, now including the freight train in the Down loop and a train of empty coal trucks in the Up loop. The wreckage then burst into flames, the obsolete wooden-bodied and gaslit Great Central Railway carriages – pressed into wartime service because of a stock shortage – went up like a tinderbox. At 6.53am Tinsley sent the 'obstruction danger' bell signal to both Gretna and Kirkpatrick, stopping all traffic and alerting others to the disaster. Four Caledonian Railway locomotives were directly involved in the collisions, the express train having been double-headed. The two that collided head on in the first impact (when the troop train hit the local train) were both written off and scrapped. The local train was headed by Cardean class 4-6-0 No. 907 while the troop train's locomotive was 4-4-0 No. 121 of the 139 Class. The two 4-4-0s of the express train, which hit the wreckage a minute later, were subsequently repaired and returned to traffic – No. 140 of the Dunalastair IV class and No. 48 of the 43 class.

THE PASSENGERS' STORIES

Lance Corporal George McGurk, who was in one of the wrecked carriages, said: "As is always the case in troop trains, we were packed together like herrings in a barrel. Some were fast asleep, and most of those who were awake were so weary that when the disaster came it caught them at a disadvantage. Some of our chaps were looking out of the windows at the time and naturally they were the first to see that something was wrong. One of the men in our carriage – Glass, I think, was his name – suddenly, and with a scared face, shouted to us: 'We're running into another train.' The words were scarcely out of his mouth before there was a terrible crash and the carriage seemed to leap into the air. We were all pitched on the floor in a heap, and one man had his neck broken by the fall, while others had arms broken, heads cut and legs twisted. I was one of the first to go down, and three other chaps all fell on top of me. They squeezed the breath out of me, but otherwise I was unhurt. The wreckage of the carriage was now dropping on us, and the cries of the men injured were heart-rending. I managed to get out from the wreckage, and, along with other uninjured men, went along the train to see what could be done.

"The scene was indescribably sickening. Beside the track were the mangled bodies of men whose death had been mercifully sudden, but pinned underneath the wreckage were scores whose agonised looks and occasional cries told of acute sufferings. Pinned underneath the steel framework of a coach, we noticed a young chap who was the baby of his regiment by the look of him. Flames were coming from the wreckage near him, and he must have been suffering terribly. Yet he was more concerned about his chum than himself. 'Don't mind about me,' he cried. 'Get Charlie out first.' Half an hour later that youngster was dragged out suffering from burns and cuts in the head. 'Is Charlie safe?' he asked. We were not sure, but we thought it best to cheer him up, so we said, 'Charlie's all right.' Then he became unconscious."

Lieutenant Laing, of the Royal Field Artillery, a well-known Glasgow man, said he was asleep at the time of the smash. He was thrown on the floor and pinned underneath the seat of the carriage. The roof collapsed, but somehow he managed to scramble out. He said that another soldier helped him to rescue five people. He said: "It was a terrible sight. We saw one man hanging by the arms with his head off, and all along the trains we could hear the groans of the wounded." Private James Neally, of the Royal Scots, said: "Many of our men were literally crushed out of all semblance to human shape." A platelayer, who arrived as part of the breakdown team, praised the efforts of the fortunate soldiers who had escaped in helping their less-fortunate comrades. He said: "There was no sign of panic. They were distributed along the line in squads and were carrying out their orders without any fuss or excitement. The patience of the injured pinned beneath the wreckage was beyond praise. One man I saw had flames gathering around him on both sides, but he was not in the least excited, and was quietly doing his best to help the men who were working to release him. Another kept chaffing the rescue party while they were striving to save him. My experience convinces me that very few of the injured perished in the flames. Those who were burned in the wreckage were dead before the flames touched them – at least in most cases."

Private Hunter, a passenger on the London express, said: "The shock of collision awoke me, and, looking out of my train, which was drawn by two engines, I saw it had dashed through the debris of a collision. The sleeping cars on the London train were telescoped, and appalling scenes were witnessed. Passengers were pinned beneath the wreckage and were burned to death. Fire broke out among the debris and emitted so terrific a heat that rescuers could not get near the unfortunate victims. Groans and piteous calls for help rent the air, the scene being ghastly and heart-rending. Many soldiers were among the dead and dying. With saws and axes, the rescuers worked with superhuman energy to save life. Bodies of the dead were laid out in an adjoining field, while the wounded lined the embankment, presenting a distressing spectacle."

Commander Oliphant, who was in charge of the naval contingent on the troop train, was seen by one of the sailors to climb on to the roof of a burning carriage to rescue a Territorial soldier. The roof gave way and the commander disappeared in a shower of sparks and was never seen again. Among 60 doctors who turned out from local towns were a Dr. Edwards, of Carlisle, who was said to have, "performed operations in circumstances of remarkable difficulty." He found that a man screaming for help had his leg pinned in the wreckage, tongues of fire were licking their way towards him, and the man's groans of agony increased every moment. In a few minutes the flames would have reached him. Dr. Edwards crept beneath the wreckage, and while a hose kept the flames back, he amputated the man's leg. The soldier was safely brought out but died later. There were several other stories of such operations. It was said that many soldiers were brought out of the wreckage alive but without arms and legs. Their coats off, the doctors worked unstintingly to treat the injured, who were carried out to them in a field adjoining the line, where they were laid on mattresses pending their removal to hospital. It has been suggested that others were so badly injured that they were shot to end their misery. In Leith, a single street, Albert Street, lost 15 of its residents in the disaster.

Help had arrived from the villages of Gretna and Springfield. Other villagers had remained behind to prepare beds for the injured. Sheets, hastily seized from the beds of nearby cottages, were being torn into strips for bandages. The fire brigade was summoned from Carlisle, but through some unfortunate confusion it was some time before they arrived. There was a further difficulty even then. The firemen could not find water. There had been a drought and the little Sark river had all but dried up. By the time a reasonable supply of water had been found, and a long hose fixed, the coaches were blackened skeletons. War at its worst could not be more awful than that scene during the interminable wait for the fire brigade. The heat in many places was too great to permit the rescuers to get near enough to be of assistance. Time and again they were beaten back, and had to watch the helpless victims die in the flames. Some of the rescuers met with accidents in the inferno themselves.

Remarkably, around 60 of the surviving officers and men of the Royal Scots were taken to Carlisle on the evening of May 22. The next morning, they went on by train to Liverpool, but on arrival there they were medically examined; all the enlisted men and one officer were declared unfit for service overseas and were returned to Edinburgh. It was reported in the *Edinburgh Weekly* that on their march from the port to the railway station some children mistook the survivors for prisoners of war. However, those regular soldiers who had survived and were declared fit sailed to Gallipoli as planned. Susan Hughes, the granddaughter of a survivor, said: "He went straight on to fight but said it was worse than anything he saw in battle." Some of the bodies of the victims were never recovered, having been wholly consumed by the fire.

When the bodies of the men of the Royal Scots were returned to Leith on May 24, 1915, they were buried together in a mass grave. The coffins were laid three deep, with each on the top row covered in the union flag. The public was excluded from the cemetery, although 50 wounded servicemen who were convalescing at a nearby military hospital were allowed to attend. The ceremony lasted three hours, at the end of which a volley of three shots was fired and the Last Post was sounded. The bodies were escorted by the 15th and 16th Battalions Royal Scots; the Edinburgh Pals battalions that had just been assembled and were still undergoing training. The cortege took four hours to complete its task. A memorial to the dead troops was erected in Rosebank Cemetery in 1916.

Of the troops, 83 bodies were identified, 82 were recovered but unrecognisable, and 50 were missing altogether. The soldiers were buried with full military honours. Among the coffins were four bodies, which were unidentified, and appeared to be remains of children. One coffin was simply labelled as "little girl, unrecognisable" and another as "three trunks, probably children." As no children were reported missing, the railway company moved the bodies to Glasgow for possible identification, but no one came forward to claim the bodies. It was speculated that they were runaways. The four were buried in Glasgow's Western Necropolis on May 26. The footplate crew of the troop train were both from Carlisle, and they were buried at Stanwix Cemetery the same day.

NINETEEN YEARS LATER: A DRIVER TELLS HIS STORY

In May 1934, David Wallace, the driver of the local train hit by the troop train, told his story for the first time in the *Sunday Express*, as follows: "The signal fell. I pulled the lever, and my train, the slow Carlisle-Glasgow train, backed quietly over the cross-over points on to the Up line. I had been driving that train for several years, but that morning – Whit Saturday, 1915 – there was a slight difference in the routine. Usually we were shunted on to a loop line at Kirkpatrick, three miles further north, to allow the London-Glasgow express to pass through. But this morning we were running late. We had to stand aside for the express earlier than usual. Our movements were regulated from the Quintinshill signal box, which stands 10 miles north of Carlisle and half a mile from Gretna Junction. It was a glorious early-summer morning, sunny and cloudless. Green vestures, dappled with trees, stretched on either side of the track.

"I remember admiring the peaceful beauty of the scene as my fireman, George Hutchinson, and I ate our breakfast, cooked over the engine fire. The gentle hissing of the engine was the only sound as we waited. The thought of anything going wrong had never occurred to us. We had picked up the Quintinshill signalman at Gretna, where he lived, and dropped him at his 'box a short distance along the line from where we now stood. We had been given the signal to pull on to the Up line, because trucks already occupied the loop lines at Quintinshill. And, fulfilling the letter of railway law, my fireman had walked along to the 'box to report our position officially. We presumed the signalman had placed the customary red 'collar' on the lever that worked the signals admitting to the line on which we stood, and so would be reminded that nothing else could come through in the meantime.

"It was Hutchinson who broke the silence. 'Dave,' he shouted suddenly, 'What's this coming?' I looked northwards. At first I could see nothing. Then I made out a thin wreath of smoke curling on the skyline. In a moment the unmistakable shape of an engine came into view. My first feeling was of amazement. I could not believe my eyes. But my surprise turned to horror in an instant. No matter how it happened, here was a train bearing down on us, on the same line. There was no scheduled train due. I knew that. Then the explanation flashed into my mind. It was the troop train. For a week, a troop train from the north had been expected on this section of the line. It was coming steadily nearer. Its roar was growing louder each second. It was doing a good 60mph for the line from Kirkpatrick to Quintinshill, which is downhill and a well-known speed run among drivers. Nothing anybody could do now could prevent disaster. 'Back, back, for God's sake,' yelled Hutchinson. I knew it was no use. We could not get out of the path of the oncoming train. The only thing I remember of the agonising seconds that followed is my leap from the footplate. Without waiting to get on to my feet, I dived under a goods truck on the loop line. I looked out from there just in time to see the collision.

"With a deafening roar the engines met. The tender of the troop train closed in like a concertina. Before my eyes the driver and fireman were forced into the furnace of their own engine. My fireman, who had jumped down on the other side of the track, saw them burn to death. The chaos was terrible. Splintered bodywork and glass flew everywhere. Men went hurtling through the air."

EVEN NOW THE WORST WAS NOT OVER
"In 90 seconds the night express from London to Glasgow – the train for which we had been shunted – was expected to pass through. I knew we could not do anything in the time. The guard of my train, Douglas Graham, had realised what was about to happen. Uninjured in the first smash, he now scrambled from his van and raced along the line. I knew he was going to make a noble but vain effort to prevent the express from coming through. I watched him, and prayed. He had not gone a hundred yards when I knew the worst."

HE WAS TOO LATE
"On the horizon to the south an ominous streamer of smoke appeared. Another moment and the express came into sight, bearing down on the piled wreckage. My frantic shouts of warning to the men on the line went almost unheard. Many of those who were uninjured were dazed or too busy attending to their injured comrades to heed my cries. Through the tangled heaps of wood and metal came the express. Man after man in its path was ploughed down. The horrors of the first crash were redoubled in the second. Grinding brakes. Splitting coachwork. Breaking glass. Hissing steam. And through it all the awful screams of the men as they fell. Then the final disaster. From the midst of the wreckage sprang a sheet of flame. Then another. The old-fashioned wooden coaches of the troop train were lit with an antiquated system of gas jets supplied from containers set between the bogies. Most of them had been damaged by the first crash. When the express came through, its two engines showered sparks on the wreckage. In a few moments the fire was raging all along the track.

"We, the survivors, had a new problem – whether to try first to extricate the injured or to attempt to quell the flames. The troop train had suffered most damage. The casualties were heaviest among the soldiers – the 7th Battalion of the Royal Scots. The passengers on the express train had been luckier. Though their coaches were smashed and every man and woman had been badly shaken, there were comparatively few casualties. Most of the passengers hurried out on to the track to help us to do what we could for the relief of the others. A group of naval men who had been aboard armed themselves with fire extinguishers and began to fight the flames. But scores of men were still trapped in the furnace. Some could not move because their limbs were jammed between the seats. Others were pinned under the wreckage. Some lay within shattered carriages, the doors of which had been locked before leaving Scotland.

"Suddenly a new alarm ran round. There was an ammunition van on the troop train," continued Wallace. "Several of us rushed up the line towards it. But before we reached it there was a series of sharp explosions. The van blew up, throwing up clouds of choking gunpowder. Fortunately, the ammunition had been so packed that the explosions were sending the missiles harmlessly upwards and not outwards. We struggled with the couplings, got them loose, and managed to push the van along the line until it was well away from the wrecked trains. The rescue work was going on steadily."

'PURE FORGETFULNESS' AND ITS DIREST CONSEQUENCES

"I shall never forget some of the things I saw," continued driver Wallace. "A woman who had been travelling in the local train was lying screaming for help in some telescoped wreckage. Her leg was caught. The flames had reached the compartment and would have been on her in another moment. There was no time for skill. A farm labourer saw the only chance to save her life. Her leg must be amputated. I shall spare you the grim details, but in his own rough way he did it, and her life was saved in the nick of time. I remember one terribly burned man begging an officer to shoot him. One by one the dead and injured were dragged from the wreckage as the fire subsided. Some of the bodies were placed in a barn not far from the track. Others were taken to Stormont Hall at Gretna, which was incongruously gay with coloured flags and bunting; decorations for a dance the previous night. Doctors were at work all over the track, easing pain as best they could, injecting morphia in the worst cases.

"Late that night the work was still going on. Nobody knew how many had died. Cranes had arrived to move the masses of wreckage from the permanent way. An attempt was made by an officer of the Royal Scots to call the roll. There had been 500 men on the train. Only 52 men answered that roll call. Some had gone off with injured comrades. Many survived their injuries. But even when the casualty list had been reduced to its minimum there were still 220 killed or missing.

DOZENS WERE UNIDENTIFIED, SOME WERE NEVER FOUND

"We found bayonets, rifles, buckles, and other equipment transformed by the fire into shapeless masses of metal. An inquiry was held almost immediately. It was revealed that the signalman who had travelled with us to his 'box had been in the habit of arriving on duty half an hour later than he ought. This was done by private arrangement with the man he was relieving. It was an irregular practice. On that Whit Saturday morning, the man due to come off duty did not leave the box at once. He stayed and read a newspaper. He had been reading extracts to the signalman who had come on my train and to one or two other colleagues who were in the 'box. It seems incredible, but the terrible disaster was down to pure forgetfulness. The diversion of the reading had made them forget that my train was blocking the Up line, with the result that the southbound troop train was given an 'all clear' signal."

Thus they went on to cause the worst railway accident in British history.

"I am told I am a lucky man. I know it. Twenty years ago, I fell from the footplate of the 'Night Scot' as it raced through Lockerbie station at 80mph. I was picked up unhurt. Two days after the Gretna disaster I had to drive a train carrying coffins for the victims. When they were being loaded, I found one was marked for me! Those four companies of the Royal Scots were dogged by bad luck. The ship carrying the survivors of the Gretna disaster was torpedoed in the Mediterranean on a later stage of their journey to the East."

BLAME SQUARELY LAID AND ACCEPTED

Lieutenant-Colonel E. Druitt RE of HM Railway Inspectorate, who headed the first investigation, which began in Carlisle's County Hall on May 25, 1915, entirely blamed both Meakin and Tinsley, who readily owned up to their failings, for the disaster. He wrote: "This disastrous collision was thus due to want of discipline on the part of the signalmen, first by changing duty at an unauthorised hour, which caused Tinsley to be occupied in writing up the Train Register Book, and so diverted his attention from his proper work, secondly by Meakin handing over the duty in a very lax manner; and, thirdly, by both signalmen neglecting to carry out various rules specially framed for preventing accidents due to forgetfulness on the part of signalmen."

Meakin should have completed his duties and then left the signal box, whereas he remained, reading a newspaper. "Although he says he did not read aloud, he admits that he may have made the other men in the 'box aware of interesting news in the paper," said Druitt. "It was to be regretted that signalmen did not look out to see if the line over which a approaching train was to run was clear of an obstacle before lowering the signals. Many collisions could be prevented if simple precaution were always taken. Had Tinsley done so, he could not have helped seeing the local train."

The inspector also said that the Gretna station master, Alexander Thorburn, who had responsibility for Quintinshill signal box, must have known about the informal shift arrangements of the pair, and also criticised fireman Hutchinson for his part. Druitt said that even if all the trains had been lit by electricity, a fire would still have occurred as the wagons of the goods train in the Down loop caught fire. He also said that had Quintinshill been equipped with track circuiting, then the accident would have been avoided as the electrical interlocking of the signals would have prevented Tinsley from pulling the relevant signal levers, but that with its simple layout and good visibility from the signal box, Quintinshill was a low priority for track circuits to be installed.

The final legal inquiry into the disaster was held on November 4, 1915 in Dumfries under the Fatal Accidents Inquiry (Scotland) Act 1895. Looking into the deaths of the crew of the troop train, and presided over by Sheriff Campion, it came to the same conclusion as the English inquest and the trial that if Meakin and Tinsley had followed the rules then the accident would not have happened. As several of the victims subsequently died in England, an inquest could also be held south of the border. Accordingly, a 19-man jury at an inquest in Carlisle heard numerous accounts of personal tragedies in the disaster. The Caledonian Railway sleeping car attendant on the express from London said that when the collision occurred, the front sleeping car was smashed and the passengers were hurled from it into the second sleeping car, which was partly smashed. A Mr and Mrs Macdonald, of London, were in the first sleeping car. Mrs Macdonald was injured and her husband, who shortly afterwards died in hospital, was thrown among the wreckage. She told rescuers: "Don't trouble about me; get my husband out. He is suffocating; I am all right."

The station master at Gretna said that both Tinsley and Meakin were "steady" men and he was not aware that they were not keeping their proper times. Robert Killin, assistant superintendent of the Caledonian Railway, said the company's rule with regard to the use by signalmen of lever collars, designed to prevent the consequences of forgetfulness, was regarded as "very important". He said that Meakin disobeyed the company's rules in not changing at the designated time. Meakin admitted he did not have permission to change other than at six o'clock. Tinsley made a remarkable admission at the inquest. He said that when he pulled the signals to allow the troop train to pass, he forgot about the local train standing on the Up main line. The jury took only an hour to decide that the passengers had died due to the gross negligence of Tinsley, Meakin and Hutchinson, and delivered a verdict of manslaughter.

In summing up, coroner T.S. Strong told the jury that in considering the case they must bear in mind that when a man had undertaken a duty which involved serious results, it was paramount that he should not treat it with indifference. It had been the duty, he said, of Meakin to have used the lever collar, and he also failed to operate the blocking back signal. Hutchinson, when he went to the signal box, failed to observe whether the lever collar was on as he ought to have done. Signalman Tinsley's part was so glaring that it was difficult to see what excuse there could be, the coroner said. He concluded his summing up as follows: "If you find as a result of your deliberations that the rules and safeguards were broken by one or more of the railwaymen concerned, or in other words that they have been negligent, there remains one point which you must decide, and it is this. Was that negligence of such a character – having regard to all the surroundings – as to be culpable negligence, or in other words gross negligence? If so it was manslaughter." That was the verdict that the jury returned.

THREE ACCUSED ON TRIAL

The coroner used his powers to commit all three to Cumberland Assizes on manslaughter charges, releasing them on bail in the meantime. Meakin was charged with having failed to place a lever collar on the handle of his lever, making the signal, which protected the main line, and having failed to give the blocking back signal that the main line was not clear. Fireman Hutchinson was charged with returning to his train from the signal box without having received the assurance that his train was protected. Tinsley was charged with culpable homicide under Scottish law and, unusually, also faced a manslaughter charge in England based on the same facts, accepting the troop train when he was aware the other passenger train was on the line. The solicitor representing the three railwaymen protested that the committing of them to trial was outside the coroner's jurisdiction, as the alleged offence had been committed in Scotland. The coroner replied that he had been instructed to proceed with the inquest by the Home Office. So the three had become the first men in history to be indicted for the same crime in two UK countries. After discussion between the Law Officers of England and Scotland, it was decided to proceed against the three men in the latter country.

At the trial in Edinburgh's High Court, which began on September 24, 1915, the three pleaded not guilty to culpable homicide and breach of duty, Tinsley claiming he had suffered a momentary memory loss. The Lord Justice General, Lord Strathclyde, presided over the trial, while the Lord Advocate, Robert Munro KC, prosecuted and the three men were defended by Condie Sandeman KC. Tinsley, Meakin and Hutchinson all pleaded not guilty to the charges of culpable homicide and breach of duty against them. The trial lasted a day and a half, and Sandeman successfully submitted to the Lord Justice General that there was no case to answer by Hutchinson. Sandeman called no witnesses on the part of Meakin and Tinsley but instead sought to persuade the jury that neither had been criminally negligent, and that Tinsley had just had a momentary loss of memory.

Concluding his summing up, the judge said: "At 6.43 on the morning of the day in question the men in the signal box at Quintinshill were asked to accept the troop train coming from the north. They accepted it. That meant that they gave the signal to the north that the line was clear and that the troop train might safely come on. At that very moment when the signal was given there was before the very eyes of the men in the signal box a local train which was obstructing the line on which the troop train was to run. One man in the signal box had actually left the train a few minutes before just at the time when it was being shunted on to the Up line. The other man had a few minutes before directing the local train to leave the Down main and go on to the Up main. That is the staggering fact that confronts you. If you can explain that fact consistently with the two men having faithfully and honestly discharged their duties you should acquit them. If you cannot explain that staggering fact consistently with the men having faithfully discharged their duties then you must convict them." The jury retired at 12.40pm but returned only eight minutes later, finding Tinsley and Meakin guilty as charged. Tinsley received three years' imprisonment and Meakin 18 months.

However, it has since been argued that the pair were made scapegoats for the railway's failure to properly plan train movements, supervise working practices and also its greed for profit regardless of safety regimes. It has been said that the level of supervision was shoddy or worse, with company rules being flouted as a matter of course across the system, but Tinsley and Meakin had to be made to pay for it. That argument was posited in a BBC television documentary, *Britain's Deadliest Railway Disaster: Quintinshill*, first aired on May 20, 2015. In the programme, the disaster was re-examined from the perspective of a modern-day rail inquiry. It argued that both signalmen had been made scapegoats for the crashes, and found fault with both the Caledonian Railway company and the government, which ran the railways during World War One. On behalf of Tinsley and Meakin, the National Union of Railwaymen appealed for clemency. However, Scottish Secretary Thomas McKinnon Wood sat for a Glasgow constituency that effectively revolved around the Caledonian Railway's works. Union leader Jimmy Thomas argued that there had been a gross miscarriage of justice but Wood was opposed to any early release.

Yet in 1916, Wood was moved to another cabinet post. The new man in the job, Harold Tennant, looked again at the sentences. By that time, even the trial judge recommended that Tinsley's sentence should be cut, but Tennant sat on his findings. Thomas then threatened a rail strike. Ten days later, the men were released. It seems astonishing in the circumstances, but after he was freed, Tinsley immediately returned to working on the Caledonian Railway as a lampman and porter at Carlisle Citadel. He died in 1961 aged 77. Furthermore, Meakin found fresh employment with the company, as a goods train guard. After he was made redundant, he became a coal merchant, trading from Quintinshill siding, next to the crash site. He also worked as a clerk at Gretna ammunition works and died in 1953. The BBC documentary mentioned above postulated that there had been some conspiracy between the company and the men to take sole blame for the accident, citing the fact both men returned to work after their sentences.

TOM ROLT'S VERDICT
In his book *Red for Danger*, transport historian Tom Rolt wrote: "Imagination can scarcely conceive what the feelings of those two unhappy men, Meakin and Tinsley, must have been when they watched, as from some grandstand, the frightful consequences of their carelessness taking place below. No punishment that any law could inflict could be more terrible, for the memory of the scene must have haunted them for the rest of their lives. Surely they are to be pitied rather than blamed, for have we not all been equally careless and forgetful on occasion but with no such fearful result?" The net result was that disaster hastened the end of gas lighting in carriages and improved and enhanced their crashworthiness.

ROYAL REMEMBRANCE A CENTURY ON
A century to the day after the crash, the tragedy was remembered by a march to

Quintinshill railway siding, the unveiling of a roll of honour at Gretna Old Parish Church, a commemorative tree planting at Gretna Green war memorial, a reading of a poem about the crash at Stormont village hall and a wreath laying at Quintinshill Bridge. The Princess Royal laid a wreath after the ecumenical service, with a second one being laid on behalf of the Royal Scots. She told one local man: "I'm really astonished at how little is known about Quintinshill." The day before, a memorial service was held in Larbert, Stirlingshire, when a procession walked from the town's parish church to the railway station, from where the troop train had departed. Princess Anne and Scottish First Minister Nicola Sturgeon also attended a service at Rosebank Cemetery in Edinburgh on March 23, 2015, attended by 100 people. Several of the relatives of those who died had travelled from overseas to attend the service at the cemetery where many of the soldiers are now buried.

In a moving ceremony on Armistice Day 2015, a rare Victorian railway carriage, of the type involved in the Quintinshill rail disaster, was dedicated to members of the Royal Scots regiment killed or injured in the disaster more than a century before. The dedicatory event, held at the heritage Great Central Railway (Nottingham), was led by the Rev. Andrew Buchanan, vicar of Ruddington, in the presence of Michael Rowen, Deputy Lord Lieutenant of Nottinghamshire, supported by the chairman of Nottinghamshire County Council, the Mayor of Rushcliffe, and members of the local Royal British Legion. Members of the Royal Scots Regiment paid their respects to their fallen colleagues of 1915, being joined by members of the volunteer team who had restored the former Manchester, Sheffield & Lincolnshire Railway six-wheeled carriage.

No. 946, built at Gorton in 1888, is one of eight Great Central carriages owned by the Ruddington-based GCR Rolling Stock Trust, a registered charity that restores vintage GCR carriages of the type that ran on the company's London Extension through Nottingham – sadly closed between 1966-69. The connection between the Quintinshill disaster and the GCR is that the troop train was partly comprised of antiquated government-requisitioned rolling stock, including several GCR vehicles of the same type as No. 946. Four similar carriages are preserved at Ingrow on the Keighley & Worth Valley Railway (an earlier four-wheeled type coach), the Midland Railway Centre at Butterley, the Chasewater Railway and the Buckinghamshire Railway Centre. The unusual dedicatory event was arranged by the trust as a tribute to the fallen of the 1st/7th (Leith) Battalion of the Royal Scots. At the ceremony, the Robin Hood Rifles Cadet Corps of Drums was complemented by the mournful laments of Piper Andrew Mackey, while Michael Rowen, Deputy Lord Lieutenant of Nottinghamshire, unveiled a commemorative brass plaque, newly attached to the carriage.

Chapter 15

1945 BOURNE END: BLINDED BY THE LIGHT

A driver's error was held responsible for an overnight sleeper express crash on the West Coast Main Line in Hertfordshire on September 30, 1945, leaving 43 people dead, one of the worst death tolls in the history of Britain's railways, and stepping up calls for Automatic Train Control systems to be introduced. There have been many major accidents resulting from stop signals passed at danger. Equally, there have been others where the indication of a distant signal or slow for a speed restriction over a set of points has been ignored. Such an instance happened with calamitous results at Bourne End near Hemel Hempstead on September 30, 1945, when the 15-coach Perth to Euston sleeper car express headed by LMS Royal Scot 4-6-0 No. 6157 *The Royal Artilleryman* and carrying 398 passengers, many of them servicemen and women, was wrecked on the four-track main line.

The express was scheduled to divert from the fast to the slow lines at Bourne End. However, owing to Sunday engineering work in Watford Tunnel, Up trains were being diverted south of Bourne End, on the LMS, switching from the Up fast to the Up slow, two tracks away on the left. There was a 20mph speed restriction on the crossover, and while it was subsequently estimated that it could have been taken safely at 40mph, No. 6157 was travelling at between 50 and 60mph. The track burst, and the locomotive and the first six carriages overturned and fell down an embankment into a field. The first vehicle, a luggage van, was completely crushed and the second carriage ended up at right angles above it. The floor of the third coach was torn out and was pointing upwards at an angle of 45 degrees. Only the last three coaches, two sleeping cars and a brake van remained on the track.

The disaster happened directly in front of Bourne End signal box. Signalman Harry Nash could only stand and watch helpless as it unfolded. The Second World War had been over for just a few weeks, but the carnage was comparable with any scene from the worst of the blitz. The alarm was raised by an American pilot, a Captain McCallum, who had just taken off from the USAAF base at Bovingdon Aerodrome and who had observed the accident during take-off and notified the railway authorities via the Bovingdon control tower. Also, a couple living in nearby Pix Farmhouse heard the hissing of escaping steam as the locomotive ran off the embankment into the field, and they called the police. The emergency services responded rapidly, and a doctor on the train gave immediate assistance where most needed, but 43 passengers, including five railway employees, died, 38 at the scene and five later.

The dead included both driver Sidney Swaby and fireman Walter Jones along with several young brides. The five railway staff who died worked on the Royal Train dining car and were travelling home as passengers. Furthermore, there were 124 others who were injured or left severely shocked. The fire brigade, airfield staff, the Red Cross, St John nurses, former Civil Defence workers, the Women's Voluntary Service and local people joined forces for the rescue operation. The injured were taken to the West Hertfordshire Hospital in Hemel Hempstead for treatment for minor injuries, shock,

One of the seminal images of rail disasters in recent times; a driving car came to rest on Potters Bar station platform, after undetected faults in points derailed it. The crash on May 10, 2002, claimed the lives of seven people. (p7) *CHRIS MILNER/THE RAILWAY MAGAZINE*

ABOVE: Christmas Eve 1874 witnessed one of the worst disasters on the Great Western Railway, close to Shipton-on-Cherwell in Oxfordshire. A 13-coach train bound for Birmingham was travelling at 40mph when the tyre of a wheel on a third-class carriage broke. The carriage left the rails before toppling down an embankment between a river and canal bridge, dragging other coaches behind it. They broke up in the field below, while three other coaches and a goods van carried on, and one fell into the Oxford Canal. The accident left 34 dead and 69 injured. The Railway Inspectorate's Colonel William Yolland led the crash investigation and chaired the subsequent Board of Trade inquiry hearing. His report highlighted several safety problems including wheel design, braking and communications along trains. The accident came in a black decade for railway accidents, ending in the Tay Bridge disaster of 1879. However, the disaster resulted in a reappraisal of braking methods and systems, which ultimately led to the fitting of continuous automatic brakes to trains, using either the Westinghouse air brake or a vacuum brake, a gargantuan step forward in terms of the railway. (p7) *ILLUSTRATED LONDON NEWS*

RIGHT: Pioneer Stockton & Darlington Railway engine *Locomotion No.1* survived a boiler explosion, which killed its driver, and is now preserved in Darlington's Head of Steam Museum. (p10) *ROBIN JONES*

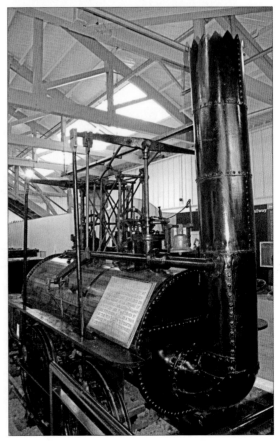

The Duke of Wellington's train and other locomotives being readied for departure during celebrations held to mark the opening of the Liverpool & Manchester Railway on September 15, 1830, which proved to be short-lived. The opening of the world's first inter-city railway was marred by the first widely reported railway death. (p10)

The National Railway Museum's working replica of Stephenson's *Rocket* and matching replica Liverpool & Manchester coaches in action on the Great Central Railway during a Golden Oldies gala on June 1, 2010. Rocket was involved in the tragedy that marred the opening day of the world's first inter-city railway. (p10) *ROBIN JONES*

Northumbrian headed the world's first ambulance train. (p10)

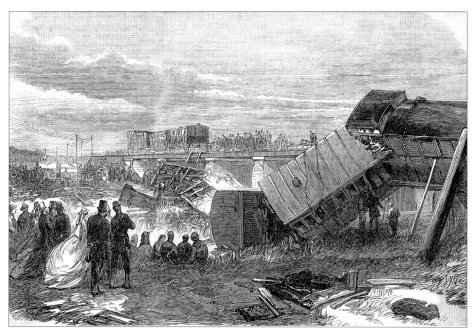

A contemporary engraving of the Staplehurst rail disaster made the day afterwards. (p18)
ILLUSTRATED LONDON NEWS

This sketch was made by Mr W.F. Callaway of Birmingham, who was on Abergele beach at the time of the accident, and saw the smoke of the burning train. He ran to the spot and remained there for several hours, making this sketch. To the right are three or four other carriages, burnt to the iron frames, but standing on the line. To the left are a few remains of the wagons, while the platelayers are at work clearing the Up line. A policeman and one of the guards, with his arm in a sling, assisted by a labourer, are examining the bodies, while other men are throwing water on the flames, passing it up in buckets from the sea. The tender, thrown on its side, with the coals in it still burning, lies across the Up line. (p21)
ILLUSTRATED LONDON NEWS

ABOVE: The wreckage of the train piled up next to the bridge. (p25)
ILLUSTRATED LONDON NEWS

LEFT: A No. 6 tablet instrument showing the restoring lever and the tablet tray in the 'out' position. (p25)
SIR ROSS BA*

ABOVE: The aftermath of the Abbots Ripton train disaster; Stirling Single No. 48 lies on its side in the snow but is otherwise undamaged. (p27)
ILLUSTRATED LONDON NEWS

LEFT: 1879 TAY BRIDGE COLLAPSE. A visualisation of the collapse of the Tay Bridge. (p31)
ILLUSTRATED LONDON NEWS

Rescuers lead the survivors from the wrecked Midland Railway race train at Hexthorpe while attempts are made to remove the dead and injured. (p37) *ILLUSTRATED LONDON NEWS*

Overturned Great Northern Railway (Ireland) 1858-built Sharp, Stewart 0-4-2 No. 9 lies on the side of the embankment at Killumney following the collision. It was repaired at Dundalk and re-entered traffic, being withdrawn and scrapped in 1915. The line lost its passenger services during the Irish railway strike of 1933, and the last section was lifted in 1955. (p40)

The wreckage of the 'Cape Mail' boat train at Norton Fitzwarren. (p43) *ILLUSTRATED LONDON NEWS*

Rescuers look for survivors in the wreckage of the sleeper train that derailed at Norton Fitzwarren on November 4, 1940. (p43) *ROBIN JONES COLLECTION*

The sleeper car in which dirty bed linen had been left next to an electric heater and started a fire that claimed the lives of 12 people. (p43)

The aftermath of the Preston accident of 1896 which, although by no means the worst of the era in terms of loss of life, sent shock waves throughout the rail industry and ended competition for increasing speed from London to Scotland for nearly four decades. (p48) *PRESTON DIGITAL ARCHIVE*

Great Western Railway Chief Mechanical Engineer George Jackson Churchward's fabled masterpiece, No. 3440 *City of Truro*, restored to running order for the centenary of its legendary but unofficial 102.3mph run with the 'Ocean Mails Express' over Wellington Bank in Somerset, approaches Dawlish Warren with a Vintage Trains' trip from Plymouth to Bristol Temple Meads on December 3, 2004. The negative public reaction towards increased speed in the wake of the 1896 Preston derailment meant that details of *City of Truro's* feat were drip-fed to the public over several years, the GWR fighting shy of publicity over it because of fears of a negative reaction. (p48) *BRIAN SHARPE*

LEFT: On April 6, 1896, the first day of public services on the Snowdon Mountain Railway, passengers and officials examine the wreckage of *Ladas* at the bottom of Cwm Glas gully after the crash, as portrayed in a contemporary sketch. (p53)

Lifting the wreckage of the three trains at Salisbury as seen on July 1, 1906. The boat train locomotive and tender jack-knifed together, killing the driver and fireman. (p55) *THE SPHERE*

Burning coaches after the triple collision; the blaze compounded Britain's worst-ever rail disaster, at Quintinshill in Dumfriesshire, on May 22, 1915, leaving 226 dead. (p57) *ILLUSTRATED LONDON NEWS*

The wreckage of a locomotive dominates the horizon after the triple collision. (p57)
ILLUSTRATED LONDON NEWS

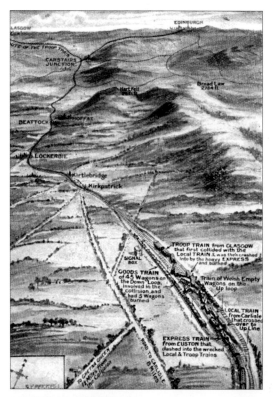

The battered No. 6157 *The Royal Artilleryman* is lowered back on to the track following the collision at Bourne End, near Hemel Hempstead, on September 30, 1945, which left 43 people dead. (p67)
C.R.L. COLES/THE RAILWAY MAGAZINE

LEFT: A contemporary diagram of how the Quintinshill disaster occurred. (p57)
ILLUSTRATED LONDON NEWS

Unlike the express train it was hauling, LNER A3 Pacific No. 66 *Merry Hampton* and its tender sustained only slight damage after falling on to soft soil. (p70)

The scene at the north end of Harrow & Wealdstone station soon after the accident on October 8, 1952, when the 8.15pm Perth to Euston express ran into the rear of the 7.31am local train from Tring to Euston, which was standing in the Up fast platform, and the 8am Euston to Liverpool and Manchester express, travelling on the Down fast line, collided with the obstruction. Its two locomotives, LMS 'Jubilee' 4-6-0 No. 45637 *Windward Islands* (pilot) and 'Princess Royal' 4-6-2 No. 46202 *Princess Anne*, and leading coaches of the Liverpool train, mounted the platform and blocked the Up electric line. (p72) *THE RAILWAY MAGAZINE*

Looking towards Euston along the fast tracks during the rescue operations, showing the damaged station footbridge and tangled mass of wreckage, under which the locomotive of the Perth train, 'Princess Coronation' 4-6-2 No. 46242 *City of Glasgow*, was completely buried. (p72) *THE RAILWAY MAGAZINE*

ABOVE: LMS Turbomotive
No. 6202, which became
Princess Anne just two months
before it was wrecked at
Harrow & Wealdstone in 1952.
(p72) *LMS*

Dedicated To The Memory Of The 17 People Who Lost Their Lives
As A Result Of The Sutton Coldfield Rail Disaster
23rd January 1955

Mr H E Allen
Mr E Blount
Mr A J Clarke
Mr S J Cleaver
Mr D Cretkovic
Mr P Hamilton
Master J A Harrison
Miss J E Harrison
Miss A Haw

Mr J Holden
Mr W Holwells
Mr J T A Howell
Mr L J Lee
Miss D Lloyd
Mr M J Newton
Mr H T Sheldon
Mrs C Wilson

And in appreciation of the people of the Royal Town
who rushed to their aid
Erected to mark the 60th anniversary of the disaster

ABOVE: On
January 24, 2016,
the day after the
61st anniversary
of the Sutton
Coldfield crash,
this plaque was
unveiled at the
station by the
Lord Mayor of
Birmingham,
Councillor Ray
Hassall. (p80)

LEFT: Railway
staff and police
working at the
site of the Sutton
Coldfield crash
on January 23,
1955. (p80)

The rail-over-rail bridge being removed from St Johns station in Lewisham four days after the collision in dense fog on December 4, 1957. The damaged bridge was being cut up to clear the lines and allow the removal of the parts of the train caught under the collapsed bridge. The temporary bridge that replaced the one in the photograph has continued in service, with some modifications, well into the 21st century. **(p83)** *BEN BROOKSBANK**

The severe damage caused to DP2 in the smash near Thirsk on July 31, 1967 in which seven passengers died. **(p86)** *JOHN M. BOYES*

Wasted because of a derailed cement wagon, this was the handsome DP2 prototype locomotive at King's Cross in 1963. (p86) *MAX BATTEN**

British Rail's Class 201 (6S) Diesel Electric Multiple Units were built in 1957-58 at Eastleigh and Ashford and were designed with a narrow body profile to accommodate the restricted tunnels on the London to Hastings line. Unit No. 1007 was leading the train involved in the Hither Green smash on November 5, 1967. Most of these 'Slim Jim' units were withdrawn and scrapped following electrification of the route in 1986. However, one complete unit, No. 1001, was preserved by Hastings Diesels Ltd., which is based at St Leonards-on-Sea. It regularly runs rail tours across the national network, and is seen at platform 8 at Liverpool Street on 1Z54, the 7.30am Hastings to Clacton-on-Sea, the 'Essex Coast Express' rail tour, on September 13, 2014. (p87) *JOSHUA BROWN**

ABOVE: Detached portion of rail as indicated by bruising on both sections, and on the broken fishplate, following the Hither Green crash on Bonfire Night, 1967. (p87)

RIGHT: The late Bee Gee Robin Gibb, a Hither Green survivor, performs on the Dutch television network AVRO programme *TopPop* in 1973. Royalties from the Bee Gees' recent UK chart hit *Massachusetts* allowed Robin Gibb, then 17, to travel first class in the train involved in the collision. (p87)

London Transport Museum's preserved 1938 tube stock set, similar to the one which crashed at Moorgate on February 28, 1975, on a private tour for sponsors on January 17, 2014. (p90) *ROBIN JONES*

ABOVE: Class 86 electric locomotive No. 86242 wedged beneath the Nuneaton station canopy following the accident on June 6, 1975. (p92) *BRITISH TRANSPORT POLICE*

LEFT: This memorial plaque is fixed to the side of Moorgate station building, in Moor Place. In July 2013, a memorial containing the names of all of those who died was unveiled in a corner of Finsbury Square, 450 yards north of the station. (p90) *ANDY MABBETT**

The wrecked Class 86 No. 86242 back on the tracks after being craned out from beneath the platform canopy. (p92) *PAUL MILLER**

Clearing up after the crash west of Clapham Junction on December 12, 1988. The numerous casualties had been brought up the bank to Spencer Park Road. (p94)
*BEN BROOKSBANK**

Memorial to the multiple train collision just outside Clapham Junction station which claimed the lives of 35 people. (p94) *ROBIN WEBSTER**

Devastation at Cowden on October 15, 1988, following a crash in thick fog which left five people dead; the remains of blue-liveried Class 205 No. 205029, which had been earmarked for preservation, lie on their side, the body having separated from its bogies. (p98) *BRIAN MORRISON*

Class 86 electric locomotive No. 86239 ended up in the garden of a house at Rickerscote, just feet from the front door, following the fatal crash on March 8, 1996. For months afterwards, the householder was still living in rented accommodation as the railway industry haggled over responsibility. (p99) *CHRIS MILNER/THE RAILWAY MAGAZINE*

The scene of the Southall disaster of September 19, 1997, seen from a passing train four days later. (p101) *BEN BROOKSBANK**

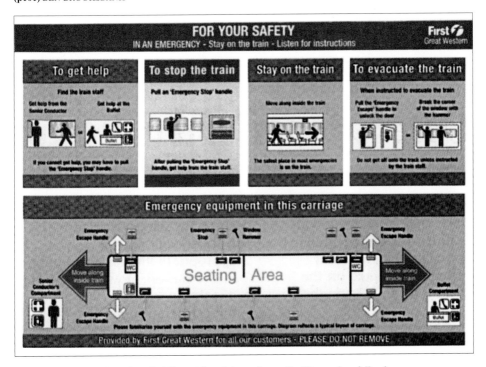

First Great Western introduced airline-style safety cards on all of its services following a recommendation by the Southall inquiry. The first of their type carried on any British train, the cards inform passengers how to escape from vehicles in the event of an accident or fire. They are carried in seat backs or on table-top clips and tell how to stop the train, how to get help and how to break windows. They also give the location of hammers and other emergency equipment. (p101)
THE RAILWAY MAGAZINE

ABOVE: The scene of devastation after a head-on collision at Ladbroke Grove on October 5, 1999 left 31 people dead. (p105) *CHRIS MILNER/THE RAILWAY MAGAZINE*

LEFT: The Ladbroke Grove crash site pictured from the air following the crash on October 5, 1999. Power car No. 43011 is seen to the right of the larger white building, while Coach H lies nearest the power car and Coaches F and G are also at oblique angles across the Up and Down main lines and the Old Oak Common depot access line, seen nearest the fence at the top of the picture. The remainder of the HST is occupying the Up main and the two remaining cars of the Turbo unit are lying on the ballast alongside them. The first coach of the DMU has disintegrated almost out of existence but its roof can be seen lying on the roof of HST Coach B, approximately level with the initial point of impact. Moving to the right, the other tracks are the Down relief, the Up relief and the tracks leading to former carriage-cleaning sidings and the Old Oak exit line. The car park of the Sainsbury's supermarket, to which many of the injured were initially taken, is on the extreme right, and the large expanse of open ground in the left centre of the photograph is where the police, rescue, forensic and breakdown recovery teams later erected their tented headquarters. (p105) *HEALTH & SAFETY EXECUTIVE*

RIGHT: Strong words displayed on a floral tribute at the scene of the Ladbroke Grove collision in 1999. (p105) *CHRIS MILNER/THE RAILWAY MAGAZINE*

MIDDLE: The crash scene near Hatfield after an InterCity 225 set derailed because of a cracked rail. (p109) *CHRIS MILNER/THE RAILWAY MAGAZINE*

BOTTOM: An aerial view of the wreckage of the trains at Great Heck on February 28, 2001. 'Dot' indicates the direction of travel, and the letters refer to the designations of the InterCity coaches for the trip. (p111) *HEALTH & SAFETY EXECUTIVE*

The wreckage of the car and its trailer after being tossed aside by the InterCity 225 unit. (p111) *HEALTH & SAFETY EXECUTIVE*

The Great Heck memorial garden alongside the East Coast Main Line. (p111) *OXANA MAHER**

The memorial garden set up alongside Potters Bar station following the crash that left seven people dead on May 10, 2002. (p115) *JULIAN WALKER**

The wreckage of the InterCity 125 High Speed Train at Ufton Nervet following the collision of November 6, 2004 after a car driver parked on the level crossing to commit suicide. (p119)
CHRIS MILNER/THE RAILWAY MAGAZINE

Twelve years after the Ufton Nervet collision which left the train driver and six passengers dead, a new £7 million bridge to replace it was finally opened on December 16, 2016. The bridge completely separates road and rail traffic at the site, which had experienced several other instances of misuse. Network Rail's regional director of infrastructure projects, Robbie Burns, was present at the opening, along with members of the Ufton Nervet survivors' support group, Great Western Railway's head of drivers, Mark Heffernan, and local councillors. The bridge project involved the relocation of the memorial garden dedicated to those who lost their lives from the south of the crossing to the north side, to join the memorial garden for Stanley Martin, the driver of the train. The level crossing is now permanently closed. (p119) *NETWORK RAIL*

Driver Stan Martin
25 June 1950 - 6 November 2004

ABOVE: On June 25, 2005, First Great Western power car No. 43139 was officially named *Driver Stan Martin*, in honour of the driver of the High Speed Train who lost his life at Ufton Nervet. (p119) *CHRIS MCKENNA*

LEFT: The Tebay accident memorial at Carnforth station. Four railway workers working on the West Coast Main Line were killed by a runaway wagon near Tebay, Cumbria, in the early hours of February 15, 2004. (p122) *STEVE DANIELS*

Derailed Virgin Pendolino unit No. 390033 *City of Glasgow* at Grayrigg on February 26, 2007. It was formally written off on November 30 that year, but the cars remaining undamaged were sent to Crewe training centre. It was not the first accident to feature a train or locomotive named *City of Glasgow* on the West Coast Main Line, as 55 years earlier, the Perth sleeper train whose crew was responsible for the Harrow & Wealdstone disaster was hauled by 'Princess Coronation' Pacific No. 46242 *City of Glasgow*. (p124) *LAWRENCE CLIFT*

Seen running down Stoke Bank on the East Coast Main Line in Lincolnshire is the Network Rail New Measurement Train, a converted InterCity Class 125 High Speed Train fitted with advanced detection and recording equipment, including scanners, lasers and digital video cameras. It can instantaneously measure and report on the condition of the track and other components. It had run over the site of the 2007 Grayrigg disaster two days before, and questions were raised as to whether its footage could have spotted the defective points. (p124) *ROBIN JONES*

fractures, and, in the more serious cases, amputations. The deceased were taken to the mortuary at Berkhamsted to await identification. Many could be identified only from personal possessions, such as rings or toys.

STRONGEST SUNSHINE OF THE YEAR

The Ministry of War Transport inquiry into the disaster was opened at Watford in October 1945 and was headed by Lieutenant-Colonel Sir Alan Mount who, with the railway officials, first visited the site. The inquiry was told that on what had been a bright autumn morning, the rising sun had been ahead of the train all the way down the long descending stretch from Tring, making observation of signals difficult. The sun was right in the driver's eyes less than 200 yards before he would have sighted the two Up Bourne End distants. Driver G. Marr, in charge of a fish train from Aberdeen which had passed the spot 50 minutes earlier, had experienced difficulty in seeing the distant signals against the sun. Marr had commented on the conditions to driver L.F. Butcher, when the latter joined the train at Watford to conduct it into Broad Street, saying that the sun was the strongest he had seen all year. Butcher and Marr did not hear about the accident till they reached Willesden 30 minutes later. However, the inspecting officer considered that the driver and fireman of the Perth train should not have failed to distinguish that the fast-line distant was showing a 'double-yellow' indication. Furthermore, the diversion had been published in the Fortnightly Notice. Top link driver Swaby and fireman Jones were based at Crewe, and Swaby was renowned for being meticulous, always reading and taking in such notices. Another contributory cause of the accident might have been the fact that the driver had been on duty on each of the previous 26 days. Swaby's son said that his sole absences from work were down to colds, and had he suffered from bouts of dizziness, diabetes, anxiety or other ailments, he would have known about them.

The district engineer stated that the whole of the crossover area at Bourne End had been entirely relaid with new metal just two years before. The LMS had adopted a programme of replacing semaphore distants with coloured lights, but at that time a double yellow could mean two very different things. One was, as now, an indication that the next signal was yellow, but at Bourne End it informed the driver that he was being diverted off the main line. This ambiguous meaning of a double-yellow distant was criticised by Lieutenant-Colonel Mount and its use was subsequently, but not immediately, banned. The role of the guard was also considered, as there was a rule, which might be interpreted as a requirement, for him to keep an eye on the driver's control of the train. However, the LMS did not consider that this was an over-riding responsibility, as it is always a difficult decision for someone back in the train. On the express the periscope provided for the guard to see signals ahead was too dirty to be of use in any case.

DEMANDS FOR AUTOMATIC TRAIN CONTROL UNHEEDED

It was presumed that the crash was down to driver error. However, the inspector told the inquiry that while he laid no blame on them, the railway companies should consider some kind of automatic train control to warn of speed restrictions ahead and, in some cases, to automatically apply the brakes. The advantages of such a system, like the type that had been in use for decades on the GWR, were stressed in his report. He stated: "Although train mileage increased during the inter-war years, the proportion of accidents (inquiry cases) which would have been prevented by this means appears to have decreased (thanks primarily to signalling improvements, track circuiting, and the introduction of coloured lights), consideration of the case for Automatic Train Control in some form remains, in my opinion, no less insistent. If the present situation is such that priority of expenditure on its installation is not felt to be justified, at least equipment of the simplest type should be objectively considered on a par with other signalling developments for application on trunk routes. It is all too easy to state a case against it on the basis that perfection and completeness are difficult of attainment; but that policy may, through fear of doing the wrong thing, lead to delay in the installation of any form of equipment.

"I recommend that the railway companies be asked to review the question with the object of initiating the introduction of Warning Control on main lines, provided the equipment is designed to conform with multiple-aspect signalling; also that the audible signal for 'clear' should not be given if speed has to be reduced." Another recommendation was that, where there was a diverging movement such as this, the signalman should keep the home signal at danger until the driver was approaching it at slow speed, and this practice was adopted at Bourne End less than three months after the accident. The crash renewed the growing, but nonetheless largely at the time unheeded, pressure on all railway companies to adopt Automatic Train Control. The debate was still ongoing more than half a century later, when further tragedies that such safety systems might have prevented occurred, again with loss of life.

Chapter 16

1947 GOSWICK: CARNAGE ON THE 'FLYING SCOTSMAN'

Two years after Bourne End, a calamity with striking similarity occurred at Goswick on the East Coast Main Line in Northumberland, when the 'Flying Scotsman' express derailed, leaving 28 people dead, in what was the last major accident before Britain's railways were nationalised on January 1, 1948.

The debate as to whether Automatic Train Control should be made mandatory was again invoked after an accident on October 26, 1947, when, like the ill-fated train at Bourne End, the 11.15am 'Flying Scotsman' express from Edinburgh to King's Cross, with around 420 passengers on board the 15 bogie coaches, failed to slow down for a diversion and came off the rails. The express, headed by LNER A3 Pacific No. 66 *Merry Hampton*, a sister engine to *Flying Scotsman* (the locomotive), had been scheduled to divert from the main fast line to a goods loop at Goswick between Berwick-upon-Tweed and Morpeth, because of engineering work. Driver T. Begbie, fireman W.R.E. Baird and train guard W. Blaikie had all failed to read the notice of the diversion posted at Haymarket depot.

As at Bourne End, the driver failed to respond to the signals in advance of the diversion and took the 15mph restricted point at around 60mph. *Merry Hampton* and most of the train then derailed and overturned. No. 66 and eight of the leading nine coaches went down the low bank into the ditch and field alongside the line, the engine and tender coming to rest on their sides in the ditch. The end six coaches remained upright and in line, the last four not leaving the rails. The fourth coach, the leading member of the triplet articulated set in the centre of the train, broke away from the train and slid for 70 yards beyond the engine and the surrounding wreckage, before coming to rest on its side across the two Up lines and also fouling the Down main line. Twenty-seven passengers and one of the train attendants lost their lives, and 59 passengers, including a naval rating, and six LNER staff, including the driver and the fireman, sustained serious injuries and were detained in hospital. Begbie sustained multiple injuries to his ribs, and Baird burns to his feet. A further 25 passengers and three of the staff were treated for lesser injuries. Begbie, an experienced driver who had been in charge of express trains between Edinburgh and Newcastle regularly for the past 12 years, was held mainly at fault. He had taken an unauthorised passenger, a naval rating, leading stoker T.A. Redden, on to the footplate, and it was thought that he may have distracted the driver's attention.

The report into the accident stated: "Having failed to see the distant signal, driver Begbie did not exercise reasonable and proper caution by a substantial reduction of speed until such time as he was in a position to be certain of all the Goswick signals. The main responsibility for this accident must therefore rest on driver Begbie. Although there is no definite evidence to confirm it, we cannot but feel that his grave breach of discipline in taking an unauthorised passenger on the footplate may well have had some bearing on his failure to exercise proper caution in the operation of his train. He is 59 years of age, and his record during his 28 years' service as driver has been fairly good; it has been clear for the last four years." Begbie claimed to have missed the distant signal because of smoke from the engine obscuring his view. The home signal was at clear to allow the train to draw up slowly to the points, but the signalman could not judge the speed of the train until it was too late, and was absolved of any blame.

In the conclusion to their report to the Ministry of Transport, Colonel A.C. Trench and Lieutenant-Colonel G.R.S. Wilson stated: "This is emphatically a case which draws attention to the value of the warning type of Automatic Train Control, giving an audible signal on the footplate and a brake application at any distant signal which is in the 'caution' position." In his report on the derailment at Bourne End in 1945, which had many features in common, Sir Alan Mount recommended that the companies be asked to review the question, with the object of initiating the introduction of warning control on main lines. "The reply of the Railway Clearing House to this recommendation referred to the system already in general use on the Great Western Railway and the experiments in hand by two of the other companies; it was pointed out, further, that apart from the question of finance, the general installation of Automatic Train Control, even of the warning type, on main lines where this does not already exist, would occupy a considerable time and employ a large number of skilled men. The supply of such staff is strictly limited, and its employment on this installation would therefore necessarily delay the execution of other work such as the modernisation of signalling, the extension of track circuiting and other similar works. This deplorable accident, however, again suggests that the installation of Automatic Train Control should be accorded high priority, and emphasises the need for a review in order that design may be agreed and a general programme prepared, for initiation as soon as circumstances allow." Lessons were still not learned; yet another call for the widespread adoption of Automatic Train Control was made, but again, it would be decades before such a system became mandatory.

Chapter 17

1952 HARROW & WEALDSTONE: BRITAIN'S WORST PEACETIME RAIL CRASH

In the morning rush hour of October 8, 1952, London's Harrow & Wealdstone station became the scene of a three-train collision that left 112 dead and 340 injured, after signals were ignored. The crash, the heaviest loss of life of any peacetime rail disaster in Britain, set in motion moves that would lead to automatic train protection.

The station was opened by the London & Birmingham Railway, later part of the West Coast Main Line, as plain Harrow on July 20, 1837. As the London conurbation expanded, it was also served by the electric Bakerloo Line. For the hordes of commuters who passed through it, it was just another station, just another means of getting into the beating heart of the capital. However, on a foggy autumn morning, all that was to change, and the station would go down in history for all the wrong reasons.

On that day, at around 8.17am, the nine-coach local Tring train stopped at Platform 4, one of the fast West Coast platforms, around seven minutes late because of fog. The train, hauled bunker first by LMS Fowler 2-6-4T No. 42389, was busier than usual because the next Tring to Euston service had been cancelled, and around 800 passengers were on board. As scheduled, this train travelled from Tring on the slow line, switching to the Up (or London bound) fast line just before the station, so as to keep the slow lines to the south clear for empty stock movements. The driver of the local train was 53-year-old A.W. Payne of Watford shed. He said that the fog was bad at Tring and although clearer through Watford and approaching Bushey, it became thicker again at Carpenders Park and Headstone Lane.

At 8.19am, just as the guard was walking back to his brake van after checking doors on the last two carriages, the 8.15pm Perth to Euston night express hauled by LMS Princess Coronation Pacific No. 46242 *City of Glasgow* – comprising 11 coaches with 85 passengers – crashed into the rear of the local train at 60mph... after it had passed a colour light signal at caution, two semaphore signals at danger, and had burst through the trailing points of the crossover from the slow lines. It had been running 80 minutes late because of the fog. Driver Payne said that his train had been standing for about two minutes when the first collision occurred, which he thought was rather longer than usual, and referred to the heavy load of passengers. He said that his train was driven forward for about an engine length by the collision and that he suffered nothing worse than bruises. However, the impact completely destroyed the rear three carriages of the local train, in which most of the casualties occurred, crushing them into the space normally taken by a single coach and pushing the train forwards by 20 yards. The front two vans and three coaches of the Perth train piled up behind and above the locomotive.

The wreckage from the initial collision was scattered across the nearby Down fast line. Then came the 8am Euston to Liverpool and Manchester express on this line, with LMS Jubilee 4-6-0 No. 45637 *Windward Islands* and Princess Royal 4-6-2 No. 46202 *Princess Anne* hauling 15 carriages with around 200 passengers. Passing through the

73

station in the opposite direction at around 60mph, the leading locomotive of this train struck the derailed locomotive of the Perth train and it too derailed. The two locomotives from the Liverpool train were diverted left, mounting the platform, which they ploughed across diagonally before landing on their sides on the nearby DC electric line. One of its electric lines was short circuited, while the other was switched off by the signalman. The leading seven coaches and a kitchen car from the Liverpool train rode over the existing wreckage piling up above and around it. The coaches impacted on the underside of the station footbridge, tearing away a steel girder. A total of 13 coaches, the kitchen car and two bogie vans were destroyed or severely damaged in the collisions, and the locomotive of the Perth train was smothered beneath the wreckage.

Survivors described hearing a deafening sound like an explosion and then broken glass and debris flying everywhere. John Bannister of Harrow was in the local train in a coach just under the footbridge at the time of the accident. He told *The Times* newspaper: "It all happened in a second. There was a terrible crash and glass and debris showered on me." He added: "I blacked out for a moment and when I came round I found I was lying on the line with debris on top of me. I managed to free myself and drag myself on to the platform." The rescue operation began immediately.

Emergency services were on the scene within three minutes, with a medical unit of the United States Air Force, based locally at RAF Northolt under Lieutenant-Colonel Weideman, giving assistance to the doctors, fire brigade, police and ambulance crews. Also playing an important role in the USAF rescue team was Nursing Lieutenant Abbie Sweetwine, who was dubbed "the Angel of Platform 6" by the *Daily Mirror*. She was later presented with an award from the people of Croxley Green for her actions. Back then, Abbie Sweetwine was a rarity indeed – for she was one of the few African-American women serving in the USAF, at a time when in many areas of the world, racial discrimination was the going rate.

Railway staff, who were working at or near the station, and railwaymen and other uninjured passengers in the local train, also undertook first aid and rescue, with Mr L. Rowlands, from the operating superintendent's department at Euston, who was in the fourth coach from the rear of the local train and was severely shaken, playing a significant role in its organisation. He also made sure that all railway departments were advised of the accident without delay. The Salvation Army, the Women's Voluntary Service and local residents also assisted where they could. The first ambulance left at 8.27am, eight minutes after the first collision, and while most of the injured had been taken to hospital by noon, the search for survivors continued until 1.30am the next day. Nurse Sweetwine carried out a simple act for which all of the receiving hospitals were grateful. She used her lipstick to mark patients. Those that had already been treated had an 'X' marked on to their forehead, while those that had been given morphine were given an 'M'. She told the ambulancemen what the marks meant, and so the hospitals were quickly able to build up a basic idea of the victims' treatment thus far, preventing overdoses of drugs and giving them a head start in identifying and treating the most critically injured.

A subsequent Metropolitan Police report praised the response from the emergency services. Co-ordination on the spot was hampered, however, by the lack of communications equipment. There was only one walkie-talkie that, in the end, was not used – and the only telephone was a walk away. The 112 dead included driver Bob Jones and fireman Colin Turnock of the Perth express, both of Crewe North shed, and the driver of the lead engine of the Liverpool train, A.J. Perkins. His fireman, G. Cowper, and the driver of the Jubilee, W. Darton and his fireman, G. Dawler, survived. All four footplatemen on the northbound train were from Liverpool Edge Hill shed. A total of 102 passengers and staff died at the scene, with 10 more dying in hospital from their injuries. At least 64 of the fatalities occurred in the local train, 23 in the Perth train, and seven in the Liverpool train. It remains uncertain as to the other 14, and it has been conjectured that some of the fatalities may have been standing on the platform and hit by the Liverpool train's locomotives. Thirty-six passengers who were killed and many of the injured were railway staff who were travelling to work in London, the majority of them in the London Midland Region offices at Euston.

Four railway staff on duty were also detained in hospital, including the fireman of the leading engine of the Liverpool train and the driver and fireman of the second engine; these three men all had remarkable escapes when their engines were overturned. Of the 340 people who reported injury, 183 people were given treatment for shock and minor injury at the station and 157 were taken to hospital, where 88 were detained. All six lines running through the station were closed, including the undamaged slow lines, to allow the injured access to ambulances. The middle section of the footbridge was cut away to free up the front two coaches of the local train, which seemed relatively undamaged. Other coaches were cut through to bring out survivors and the dead. Policemen occasionally shouted or blew their whistles for silence to listen for any signs of survivors in the wreckage. The slow lines reopened at 5.32am the following day, while the electric lines were used by cranes to remove the Liverpool locomotives and carriages and reopened on the afternoon of October 11. The fast lines were reopened, with a speed restriction, on October 12. The Queen and the Prime Minister, Winston Churchill, sent messages of sympathy to the victims and the bereaved.

WHO WAS TO BLAME?

The inquiry into the disaster opened at Euston station on October 15, 1952, and on June 12 the following year, the Ministry of Transport published its report on the collision. Written by Lieutenant-Colonel G.R.S. Wilson, it reiterated the fact that the Tring train should have been protected by two semaphore home signals; the Up Fast Inner Home about 190 yards to its rear, and the Up Fast Outer Home 440 yards further back. A colour distant signal (the Up Fast Distant) would show green if the Outer Home was at 'clear' or yellow if the Outer Home was at 'danger' and was set 1,474 yards before the Up Fast Outer Home, the full braking distance for a 75mph express adhering to the speed limit at this location. Tests had shown that there was nothing wrong with the signalling. Neither did the signalman change the route after the Perth express had passed the caution signal. It was found that the driver of the Perth train had not slowed his train in response to this signal. He had then passed two danger signals before colliding with the Tring train. It seemed that the driver, Jones, had made no attempt to stop until the very last moment. That assumption was corroborated by survivors on board the Perth express who said that the emergency brake was applied a few seconds before the collision. Jones was still gripping the brake lever when his body was found.

The 61-year-old guard, J. Kent, who was stationed at Carlisle, had described the running of the train. After working from Carlisle with another train, Kent had joined the Perth train at Crewe, where he had given driver Jones the usual information about the load, and had passed instructions to him to make special stops at Nuneaton and Rugby, which were part of the train service alterations on account of the re-signalling work at Euston. He said that Jones had seemed in good health when he had spoken to him and had remarked on the fog and difficulty he had had in backing on to the train; he had not, however, displayed the least anxiety about the journey and had told Kent that he would do his best in the circumstances. Kent said that after leaving Crewe at 4.37am, 32 minutes late, the train continued to lose time and he thought that this was down in the main to the driver, "finding his signals" in the fog. His journal recorded signal checks at Baddesley and at Atherstone (between Stafford and Nuneaton), also at Watford Tunnel (North End), and he said that the brake had operated normally on all these occasions, as well as at the special stops at Nuneaton and Rugby. He said that speed restrictions at Watford Tunnel North End had been strictly observed. He related that he had begun to tie up his invoices into bundles to be thrown out into the net at Camden Goods Yard, and he mentioned that he had a good deal more invoices and letters than usual owing to the train alterations. The train was "just getting into its swing again" when the collision occurred, he had said.

He thought that the express might have been travelling at 50-55mph. The first indication to him that something was wrong was a severe application of the brake, and he had noted that his van vacuum gauge had gone to zero almost instantaneously. This brake application was followed by a five-second interval then three violent forward lurches and an equally violent rebound. His impression was that the driver "had spotted something just too late".

Kent was not injured, and had alighted from the train with a red flag and detonators with the intention of protecting the Up fast line, but he was quite close to the signal box and went there first of all. The signalman, who appeared to "have had a shaking", had told him that all lines had been protected, so he went round to the off side to make sure of the Down fast line, and was surprised to see that the Liverpool train had already run into the wreckage. Kent said that he had looked sideways through the window of his van once or twice between Watford and Harrow and described the visibility generally as "not dense but patchy". He did not think it was bad enough to have fogmen out, though he remembered having heard their detonators between Crewe and Rugby.

On this part of the line at peak times, local trains had priority over expresses. Therefore, the crew of the Perth express should have expected the signals to be against them. The driver, said to be 'a methodical young man', was in good health; there was no evidence of a medical problem or equipment fault that would have distracted him at that point. Could he have mistaken the green colour signals on the adjacent electric lines for the Up Fast Distant, or had the low sun impaired the signalling, it was asked. The report ruled out both possibilities. While the fog had lifted around the station, with visibility improving to 200-300 yards, witnesses estimated the visibility at the Up Fast Distant to have been 50-100 yards. For a train travelling at 50mph, that distance would be covered in four seconds at the most.

The report said that the driver, "must have relaxed his concentration on the signals for some unexplained reason, which may have been quite trivial, at any rate during the few seconds for which the Distant signal could have been seen from the engine at the speed he was running in a deceptive patch of denser fog. Having therefore missed the Distant he may have continued forward past Headstone Lane station (which was not on his own side), underestimating the distance he had run from Hatch End and still expecting to see the colour light and not the Harrow semaphore stop signals which were at a considerably higher elevation." Colleagues thought of driver Jones, 43, as a careful and conscientious driver. He started on the railway in 1927 as a cleaner and worked his way up through the links. He passed out as a driver with high marks in 1948 and was familiar with most of the routes out of Crewe including the fast run down to Euston, a journey he had made nearly 30 times before.

Fireman Turnock, 23, had joined the railways as a bar boy in 1943, becoming a cleaner the following year and a fireman in 1945, despite still being only 16. Considered also to be conscientious, he was well on the way to becoming a driver himself and had fired London expresses more than 30 times previously. Nobody has ever been able to establish why Jones and Turnock did not stop at the well-positioned signals, which were found by investigators to have been working properly. They both knew the line and when to expect the signals. The accident report tentatively concluded that somehow Jones had missed the Distant, either through a sudden wisp of the remaining fog or possibly the remains of the smoke from a passing freight train. Then, still looking for the Distant (which was deliberately positioned at driver eye level), he somehow missed the Outer Home, which being a traditional semaphore-style signal was higher up, as well.

The report highlighted the fact that there had been only eight deaths in the leading seven passenger coaches of the Liverpool express. Several of them were of the new British Railways Mk.1 type, which had been introduced in 1951, with all-steel construction, with buck-eye couplings and bodies welded to the underframe. While the newly nationalised railway had inherited coaches from the Big Four companies, it set out to produce a standard type for universal use across the system. The Mk.1 not only incorporated the best features of each of the former companies' types, but was also designed to be much stronger than previous designs, to provide better protection for passengers in accidents. The Harrow & Wealdstone disaster proved that this was indeed the case.

CLEAR ROAD AHEAD

The report said that there was no point in imposing more restrictive working practices to take into account driver error, but a far more effective solution was at hand. It said: "The way to guard against the exceptional case of human failure of the kind which occurred at Harrow does not lie in making the regulations more restrictive, with consequent adverse effect on traffic movement, but in reinforcing the vigilance of drivers by apparatus which provides a positive link between the wayside signals and the footplate." That paved the way for the future of railway networks everywhere – automatic warning systems. It was stated that if a system warning drivers that they had passed a signal at caution or danger had been adopted long before, it would have prevented 10% of the accidents and 28% of the deaths in the previous 41 years. Such a system would have saved 399 lives, including the Harrow & Wealdstone victims.

At the time, British Railways was developing an 'automatic train control' that warned drivers of an adverse signal and automatically applied the brakes, until this was cancelled by the driver. Indeed, by the time the report was published, a five-year plan had been agreed to install this system on an initial 1,332 miles of track. The inspector's report concluded: "In the regulation and execution of an Automatic Train Control programme in relation to the many other calls on the Signal Department for new work and maintenance, much must be left to the judgment of the management. I do not, however, look on Automatic Train Control as a competitor to other signalling development, but as complementary to it, as indeed was the view of the Railway Executive in 1948, when it recommended that a more extensive programme than that now proposed should be completed in six years, and that it should run concurrently with a programme of the same order for the extension of track circuiting and block controls. I would also emphasise that, in contrast to the many effective devices which have been developed and so widely installed over the years to assist signalmen in their work, the safety of traffic on the majority of our lines still depends on the personal vigilance of the enginemen, as in the earliest days. The very occasional failures which have occurred give no grounds for loss of confidence in British railway engine drivers as a whole, and there is no reason to believe that the problem has become more urgent in the last few years, notwithstanding the exceptionally tragic results of one such failure at Harrow.

"All, however, are agreed that enginemen should be given their share of technical aids to safe working, and I consider that at this late stage there should be no reservations on the rate of progress once the apparatus has been approved. I therefore recommend that all the resources which are available to the railways for the purpose should be directed to the timely accomplishment of the five-year plan and its subsequent extension as proposed, without prejudice to other necessary signalling work. The estimated first and recurring costs are large, but in my opinion the expenditure should be faced without hesitation, and no financial considerations should be allowed to stand in the way of an ambitious programme, in view especially of the arduous railway conditions in this country with its dense traffic, high speeds and adverse climate in the winter months."

Automatic Warning Systems were not a new idea – the Great Western Railway had used it since about 1905 and it had been recommended by a government committee that similar systems be adopted by all Britain's railway companies. However, uptake had been slow. Railway decision makers had by and large taken the view that while experienced cautious drivers and signallers followed the rules and signalling equipment was up to scratch, major disasters could be avoided. It was argued by many that accidents such as Quintinshill were the result of failures of men and machines, which AWS would not necessarily rectify. Yet Harrow & Wealdstone proved that AWS would have saved the day. The subsequent investigation collected a mountain of evidence that the signalmen on duty could have done no more to prevent the disaster, and neither was their equipment at fault. Apart from the 112 persons who lost their lives at Harrow, only one passenger was killed in an accident involving a train in 1952.

THE FATE OF THE THREE LOCOMOTIVES

Despite the severe damage to No. 46242 *City of Glasgow* it was rebuilt. Having emerged from Crewe Works in May 1940, it was withdrawn from Polmadie shed in October 1963 and scrapped. However, the locomotives hauling the Liverpool train were both scrapped as a result of the collision. No. 45637 *Windward Islands* was officially withdrawn on December 13, 1952 after having been condemned. The mangled remains of No. 46202 *Princess Anne* were stored until about 1954 before it was decided to scrap it, rather than rebuild it. As *Princess Anne*, that locomotive had been in existence only for two months. It had been rebuilt as a Princess Royal class 4-6-2 from a one-off experimental locomotive, William Stanier's Turbomotive. The Turbomotive was a modified Princess Royal class which, built in 1935 with the aid of the Swedish Ljungstrom turbine company, used turbines instead of cylinders. It was numbered 6202, in sequence with the Princess Royals. Although broadly similar to the other Princess Royals, it had a larger 40-element superheater to give a higher steam temperature, more suitable for turbine use. The design was not taken up for a production class, and it was rebuilt using new mainframes and a spare set of cylinders from a Coronation class locomotive. Nameplates from both *Windward Islands* and *Princess Anne* were acquired by the Doncaster Grammar School Railway Society, and remain at the school. LMS Fowler 2-6-4T No. 42389, which was built in June 1933, and was shedded at Watford at the time of the crash, was withdrawn from Speke Junction shed at Liverpool on March 23, 1963, and subsequently scrapped.

THE RISE OF A PHOENIX ENGINE

The scrapping of *Princess Anne* left the London Midland Region short of an express passenger locomotive, and so it was decided to build a new one. BR Standard 8P Pacific

No. 71000, which was outshopped by Crewe Works in 1954, was unique in several respects. Firstly, it was the only member of the 12th class of British Railways Standard locomotive to be built. Secondly, it brought to an end a long lineage of British steam locomotive development, which began with Richard Trevithick at Ironbridge in 1802. It was not the last steam locomotive to be built by BR – that was 9F 2-10-0 No. 92220 *Evening Star* at Swindon in 1960 – but it was the final UK standard gauge design. Based on the BR Standard 7P Britannia design, it incorporated three sets of modified Caprotti valve gear, which was relatively new to British locomotive engineering, and more efficient than Walschaerts or Stephenson valve gear.

However, locomotive crews regarded it negatively because of its poor steaming characteristics and heavy fuel consumption. Trials reported problems with the poor draughting of the locomotive resulting in difficulty adhering to the timetables. There was, however, a reluctance to make improvements to the locomotive, because after the 1955 Modernisation Plan was published by British Railways, calling for the eradication of steam and its replacement by diesel and electric traction, no further examples were to be built. *Duke of Gloucester* was withdrawn in December 1962 after only eight years in traffic, and, happily for history, was sent to Woodham Brothers' Barry scrapyard, where owner Dai Woodham had made a landmark decision to hold off cutting up the vast rows of redundant BR steam locomotives in favour of the more lucrative wagon scrapping business. That breathing space made a priceless and immense contribution to British transport heritage, for it allowed the nascent railway preservation movement a quarter of a century to buy 213 steam locomotives from Barry.

Among those was *Duke of Gloucester*, which because of its uniqueness, and place in the history of British locomotive development, was initially selected to be saved as part of the National Collection. However, it was later decided that only the cylinder arrangement was of interest, and one of the outside cylinders was removed for display at the Science Museum. Its cannibalisation meant that it was overlooked for private preservation until 1974, when a group of enthusiasts bought it under the banner of the Duke of Gloucester Steam Locomotive Trust. Many expensive new parts had to be made, including the Caprotti valve gear, and it would be 1986 before No. 71000 steamed again. However, during its rebuilding, enthusiasts noted two major construction errors in that the chimney was too small compared with other locomotives of similar size, resulting in poor boiler draughting, and that the fire grate air inlet dampers had not been built to the drawings and were also too small, resulting in poor air supply and inefficient combustion. Had BR engineers rectified the problem back in the 1950s, the locomotive's performance would have been dramatically improved.

These errors were corrected and the opportunity taken to incorporate some other improvements, including the previously recommended Kylchap exhaust system, which in the heritage era unlocked the *Duke*'s true potential as a powerful express passenger engine. When it was first allowed to haul a full load back on the main line, the boiler produced steam at a more efficient rate, so enthusiasts had succeeded where BR had failed or shown indifference. *Duke of Gloucester* was transformed from a failure to one of the most powerful steam locomotives ever to run on Britain's railways, and in its own indirect way, is also a memorial to the Harrow & Wealdstone disaster, to which it owes its existence. At the time of writing, no. 71000 is undergoing a major overhaul at Tyseley Locomotive Works in Birmingham.

THE RAIL INDUSTRY REACTS
The accident accelerated the introduction of British Railways' Automatic Warning System,

despite calls for more track circuits and colour light signals to be introduced instead. However, a quarter of a century would pass before a third of the national network was fitted with AWS. It was also said after the accident that the layout of the track at Harrow & Wealdstone should be altered. In 1952, it was arranged with the junction between slow and fast lines to the north of the station so the Tring train had to wait on the fast line. The junction was changed 10 years later. The accident also reinforced the case for replacing Big Four coaching stock with BR Mk.1s.

The disaster also provided for the establishment of civil disaster plans by Britain's local councils, and their regular testing. After the crash, control of the site was fragmented, with railwaymen, councilmen, police and firemen all trying their best to work together without really knowing who was officially in charge or who should be doing what. Emergency planning would go a long way to improving such situations. The disaster also led many ambulance services to look at introducing and developing the role of the paramedic, who could treat casualties on the scene, rather than having a simple 'pick up and collect' procedure. Furthermore, the heroism of black Nursing Lieutenant Abbie Sweetwine, in Harrow's hour of need and the ensuing brief period of minor fame, placed a chink in the armour of the racial prejudice of the day, as she was given her 15 minutes of fame in the national media, debunking the widespread misconception that ethnic people were less capable of doing jobs with such responsibility.

REMEMBERING THE TERRIBLE DAY HALF A CENTURY ON
A memorial plaque was placed above the main entrance on the eastern side of the station to mark the 50th anniversary in 2002. A mural was painted along the bordering road featuring scenes from Wealdstone's history by children from local schools and dedicated to the victims' memory. On October 8, 2012, local people, including witnesses to the crash and relatives of the victims, gathered at the station for a service to remember the terrible events of 60 years before. Dignitaries from Harrow Borough Council, Harrow West MP Gareth Thomas, London Underground Bakerloo line performance manager Dave Proffitt and Borough Commander Dal Babu were among those who paid their respects. Also attending were representatives of several organisations that helped with the rescue work on the day, including St John Ambulance, the Royal British Legion, the Red Cross and the Salvation Army. A drama group dressed in 1950s outfits recreated the feel of the times and sang the hymn *Abide With Me*. More plaques were laid, and, at a reception at Harrow Civic Centre for those attending the service, newsreel film showing the horror of the crash was screened.

Chapter 18

1955 SUTTON COLDFIELD: SHARP TURN TAKEN AT DOUBLE SPEED

The Sutton Coldfield crash of 1955 led to what might seem to us today a common-sense approach – the installation of speed-limit warning signs throughout the rail network. On the afternoon of Sunday, January 23, 1955, Sutton Coldfield station (in what was then still Warwickshire but now the West Midlands) experienced the worst outcome of taking a train on a sharp curve at twice the permitted speed. Seventeen people including the footplate crew lost their lives, and another 40 were injured. The 12.15pm 10-coach York to Bristol express headed by LMS 'Black Five' No. 45274, and with around 300 passengers on board, approached the station at a speed of between 55 and 60mph. The limit at that point was 30mph.When it reached the sharp curve immediately before the station, the train came off the rails and collided with the platforms. The locomotive, coaches, station buildings and carriages were badly damaged. The fourth carriage was knocked into the air causing it to drag along the station roof, damaging both the roof and the platforms to either side. The first coach was crushed between No. 45274 and the second carriage. The line through Sutton Coldfield was, and still is, normally used by suburban trains, as part of the Cross-City line. However, on this occasion, the express had been diverted away from the normal route into Birmingham via Tamworth because of engineering work.

The regular driver, 63-year-old J.T. Martin of Gloucester shed, did not know the diversionary route via Sutton Coldfield, so another driver, 54-year-old H.E. Allen of Burton (Horninglow) shed, who did, came on board at Burton-on-Trent to guide him. Driver Martin, who had worked a northbound express from Gloucester that morning via Sutton Coldfield, complained that the rough riding of the engine was tiring him. He left the footplate and took a seat in the train, leaving the conductor driver in charge. In addition to driver Allen and fireman J.T.A. Howell, also from Gloucester motive power depot, 12 passengers were killed outright, and two passengers and another driver travelling on duty subsequently died of their injuries in hospital. It is probable that Marine H. Swam, a passenger in the derailed train, who dialled 999 from a public telephone after he had forced his way out of the locked station, sent the first call for emergency assistance. The derailment blocked both lines through the station. As the signal box was switched out of circuit, all the Sutton Coldfield signals were clear, and with no local passenger service over the line on Sundays, the station was closed and unattended.

THE HEROES WHO STOPPED A SECOND COLLISION

The 1.20pm express train from Bristol to York was already in the section on the Down line, but it was stopped at the home signal well clear of the wreckage thanks to the efforts of train ticket collector G.A. Attenborough and fireman D.H. Smith who were travelling on the derailed train. Despite the fact that they had been injured and shocked by the accident, they raised the alarm to other stations, changed the signals to danger and placed detonators on the tracks to warn oncoming trains. If it had not been for their actions, the death toll may well have been much higher. Two locals, a Mr and Mrs Fairey, also ran up the line to stop trains heading towards the crash site. The Bristol to York express was eventually drawn back to Birmingham with uninjured passengers from the derailed train, some of whom continued their journey in a special train that left Birmingham at 7.32pm after refreshments had been provided. Birmingham Accident Hospital attended the crash with a mobile surgical unit as well as 40 additional ambulances from surrounding districts. RAF servicemen from Whitehouse Common provided aid to the emergency services. A temporary morgue was set up to deal with the volume of bodies being taken from the wreckage.

Most of the injured went to Sutton Coldfield's Good Hope Hospital, with Birmingham General and the Accident Hospital also taking casualties. A total of 23 passengers were detained, some with very serious injuries, along with a goods guard, who was travelling on duty. Driver Martin received facial injuries and severe shock for which he was detained in hospital for a considerable time. Twenty-four others complained of minor injuries or shock. Seventeen people were discharged the same afternoon after treatment. Wolverhampton Wanderers' player Bobby Thomson had been expected to take the train that crashed, along with six other Molineux players, Colin Tether, Dick Calvert, Harry Middleton, Stan Round, Cyril Bevan and Geoff Sidebottom. As luck had it, manager Stan Cullis called a meeting for the Sunday and the players travelled back on the Saturday instead.

Four heavy steam breakdown cranes from Saltley, Bescot, Rugby and Crewe arrived between 7pm and 9pm, but the work of clearing the site was slow and laborious, as it was necessary for the most part to work the cranes end on to the wreckage between the platforms, and to relay the track piecemeal as the formation was cleared by successive lifts. Difficulty was also experienced in making a firm base for the cranes on the clay subsoil. Fire crews remained on duty to keep the cranes supplied with water. All trains through Sutton Coldfield were suspended for the next two days, when local passenger traffic was covered by special road services during these two days. The Up and Down Lines through the station were finally restored to traffic shortly before 7am on the Wednesday.

THE NEED FOR LINESIDE SPEED LIMITS

It was easy to blame the crash on excessive speed, but because the driver and fireman had died, the exact cause of the tragedy was never established. Indeed, the driver knew the diversionary route well and at the time of the crash, it was broad daylight with excellent weather conditions. Neither was there any evidence of mechanical failure. The action of the regular driver in leaving the conductor driver in charge was criticised by inquiry chairman Lieutenant-Colonel G.R.S. Wilson, who held that even though driver Martin did not know the route, the safety of the train was still his responsibility.

At the inquiry, Martin, in excusing himself for contravening Rule 127 by leaving the footplate at Lichfield for a seat in the middle of the leading coach, referred to a leg muscle injury, which he had sustained while turning an engine on a turntable about two years previously. The injury had left him with some weakness in the leg and as the knocking of the engine was making it rather painful for him to stand, he sat down in the compartment until he could sit at the engine controls again. He knew that this was against the rule, but he said that he was thinking of his own personal comfort and the fact that he would have to carry on with the train from Birmingham. Lieutenant-Colonel Wilson said: "The speed of the engine was not far from the overturning speed on the sharp knuckle of 8¼ chains' radius at the beginning of the curve, and it was higher than the theoretical speed of derailment by flange mounting.

"The excess of speed was too great to be accounted for by misjudgment, and I can only conclude that driver Allen made no attempt to observe the 30mph restriction through Sutton Coldfield; there is also no doubt that the speed of the train through the section from Four Oaks was much higher than the 40mph laid down. It is indeed difficult to explain this extraordinary lapse on the part of a driver with such a long record of trustworthy service and who had an intimate knowledge of all the characteristics of the route. There is at least a strong possibility that the accident would have been prevented by lineside speed restriction notices or signs, acting either as a direct reminder to driver Allen on the afternoon in question, or indirectly by impressing the location and severity of the restrictions firmly in his mind as he passed the signs regularly during his working of stopping passenger trains over the route. Speed restriction signs have not been a general feature of British practice in the past, though some of the former companies, notably the Great Western, provided illuminated notices of various types at places where it was considered that a speed restriction required special emphasis or where there were no distinctive physical landmarks by which a driver could locate himself accurately."

Various theories for the exact cause of the disaster were offered. The train was running late and making up time, there was a gradient to climb after the station which was best approached at full speed, the 'Black Five', like most other engines of the day, did not have a speedometer, and was riding roughly, which may have contributed to the driver misjudging his speed. Maybe, as with the Salisbury station crash in 1906, the driver knew he was exceeding the speed limit but did not realise the extent of the danger. Lieutenant-Colonel Wilson said: "The train was still 10 minutes late when it started again from Lichfield. This was the first express Allen had driven over the route for six months, and it may be that in his anxiety to regain further time on the journey to Birmingham, or even to keep to the very sharp 15-minute booking between Lichfield and Sutton Coldfield, the speed restrictions which required no special action with stopping trains passed completely out of his mind. Though there can be no certainty in the matter, I think this is a possible explanation of what occurred." After the Sutton Coldfield crash, lineside speed restriction signs were universally adopted. Hitherto, there had been no visual reminder to the driver of speed restrictions on many routes on the UK network. The inspector also suggested the use of speed recorders as in France, but this was not adopted.

Chapter 19

1957 LEWISHAM: CARNAGE IN
THE LONDON FOG

A dense fog descended over London on the evening of December 4, 1957, and caused numerous trains to run late. The 5.18pm Charing Cross to Hayes, comprising electric multiple units totalling 10 cars and carrying nearly 1,500 passengers, stopped at a red signal at Parks Bridge Junction on the Lewisham bypass line, beneath a bridge carrying the Nunhead-Lewisham line above the four tracks. The fog upset the running order of scheduled trains, and the Parks Bridge Junction signalman wanted to speak to the driver by the telephone at the signal to confirm the train's identity and destination.

However, at around 6.20pm, a steam-hauled 11-coach service from Cannon Street to Ramsgate, hauled by Bulleid Battle of Britain Pacific No. 34066 *Spitfire*, driven by 62-year-old William Trew, and carrying about 700 passengers, was travelling at about 35mph when it collided with the rear of the stationary EMU – 138 yards after passing the red aspect of the Down through colour light inner home signal of St John's signal box. Trew failed to spot two yellow cautions approaching St John's, although he did see the red signal at the far end of the platform and braked, but *Spitfire* was still travelling at speed. The air brakes of the electric train had been applied to hold it stationary on the rising gradient. That made the shock of the collision more severe than it otherwise would have been, and the eighth coach was completely destroyed when the underframe and body of the ninth coach were forced over and through it. The impact hurled *Spitfire*'s tender and leading coach off the track, dislodging a steel middle column supporting two of the four heavy girders of the overbridge, causing it to fall on to two coaches and crush them.

Just two minutes later, an eight-coach electric train from Holborn Viaduct to Dartford, which was moving slowly on to the bridge towards a signal at red, managed in the nick of time to stop short after the motorman saw the girders at an angle. There was no damage to this train, although its leading carriage was tilted. The crash killed 90 passengers (including 37 in the EMU and 49 on the steam train); the guard of the electric train was killed outright, while another passenger died later of his injuries. The first emergency service vehicles arrived at 6.25pm with the fire brigade, ambulance and police being assisted by doctors and nurses. Help was accepted from the Salvation Army, the Women's Voluntary Service, St John Ambulance and local residents.

By 10.30pm, all of the 173 injured had been taken to hospital, with 109 detained there. Driver Trew was taken to hospital with severe shock but was allowed to make his own way home to Ramsgate on December 5. Two days later, he was interviewed in bed by the Ashford District motive power superintendent, F.L. Howard, who found it difficult to get any coherent statement from him. All four of the running lines under the bridge and the two over it were blocked. An emergency timetable started at 6.10am the following day, with local trains travelling through Lewisham, avoiding the accident, with the current switched off on the North Kent line to allow the wreckage to be cleared, and main line services diverted to London Victoria. By 4pm on December 9, the wrecked carriages and the fallen bridge had been cut up and removed. The track was then re-laid and the lines beneath the bridge reopened at 5am on December 12. A temporary bridge allowed the overhead line to be reopened at 6am a month after the crash.

DRIVER TREW ON TRIAL TWICE

Witnesses were interviewed, the visibility of the signals on the line examined, and tests showed no fault in the signalling equipment. At the subsequent inquest, the jury declared that the deaths were down to gross negligence. However, the coroner rejected the verdict and substituted one of accidental death. Driver Trew, who had had 45 years' service with the railway, including 18 as driver, and had worked with the same fireman for two years at Ramsgate shed, was blamed for the crash. Accordingly, Trew was tried for the manslaughter of the EMU guard, Robert Reynolds, at the Old Bailey on April 21, 1958. But the jury failed to agree a verdict and after a second trial he was discharged owing to severe stress-induced mental illness.

Henry Chadwick, a member of the public who assisted at the crash, successfully sued British Railways for the 'nervous shock' he experienced. The case, Chadwick v British Railways Board, set an important legal precedent, which lasted for 30 years. The court heard that after helping at the accident scene, Chadwick had become ill with an anxiety disorder and required hospital treatment. He was no longer able to work and no longer took any interest or pleasure in activities with which he had once been highly involved. He died in 1962 for causes unrelated to the accident. The court found in favour of Chadwick on the grounds, among others, that injury by shock to a rescuer, physically unhurt, was reasonably foreseeable, and the fact that the risk run by a rescuer was not exactly the same as that run by a passenger did not deprive the rescuer of his remedy.

THE DRIVER WHO STOPPED JUST FEET AWAY

The driver of the train, which stopped short of the damaged bridge with nearly 1,000 passengers on board, later recounted that terrible fogbound night. Donald Corke, who was 29 at the time, said: "In those days, there were no automatic brakes or signals. You really had to rely on your senses completely. The visibility was very, very bad and I was looking out for a red signal – I was sure there would be one," he said, at that time still oblivious to the carnage that had just taken place below. "As we came on to the bridge, I suddenly noticed the metal girder on the bridge bending upwards towards the carriage. I immediately thought the bridge must have fallen down, and applied the brakes. I wasn't scared, I just had to get on with stopping the train. When I looked down, I couldn't see anything because the fog was so thick. And there wasn't a sound coming from the wreck – the fog had muffled any noise. You could have heard a pin drop." Driver Corke's actions in stopping his train were credited with saving many lives. Had it proceeded on to that warped bridge, it is likely that the death toll would have been far higher. He retired in 1992, and, in 2003, was invited to unveil a plaque outside Lewisham train station commemorating the tragedy.

After Lewisham, British Railways was again publicly criticised for not speeding up the installation of the Automatic Warning System that would have prevented the crash. Following on from the inspector's report into the Harrow & Wealdstone disaster, the Lewisham report accelerated the introduction of the Advanced Warning System, which gave the driver an in-cab indication of signal aspect, and applied the brakes automatically in the event of a signal overrun. Yet, as we will see in Chapter 27, AWS was still not mandatory when the Southall rail crash occurred 40 years later.

The Ministry of Transport report on the crash was published in 1958. The inspector found that driver Trew had not slowed for two caution signals, and applied the brakes only after the fireman, C.D. Hoare, had alerted him that he had a danger signal. Although Trew had poor visibility of signals from the driver's seat, he did not cross over to see them, or ask the fireman to look for them. The report concluded that an "Automatic Train Control of the Warning type" would have prevented the collision. Although the installation of such apparatus had been agreed after the Harrow & Wealdstone rail crash in 1952, priority was being given to main line routes controlled by semaphore signals. The poor visibility of signals from No. 34066 was mentioned with a recommendation that the type should be fitted with wider windscreens.

On December 2, 2007, relatives of the victims gathered at a memorial service at St John's Church in St John's Vale, Lewisham, to remember them half a century on. Lewisham mayor Sir Steve Bullock said: "The effects of that day had a profound impact on the lives of so many people. It was an awful tragedy."

Chapter 20

1967 THIRSK: DERAILED CEMENT
WAGON WRECKS A PROTOTYPE

The only prototype locomotive to be written off in a serious collision and derailment was DP2, the English Electric forerunner of the Class 50s. Built at Vulcan Foundry in Newton-le-Willows in 1962, and loosely based on a Deltic bodyshell, the Co-Co was tested on the main line in May that year and on regular London Midland Region services out of Euston. Repainted in two-tone green Deltic livery, it was used on the 'Sheffield Pullman' workings until 1966. In August 1966, it was derailed at Edinburgh Waverley station, but far worse was to come. On July 31, 1967 it was involved in a serious accident at Thirsk, colliding at speed with the derailed daily Cliffe (Kent) to Uddingston (Glasgow) cement train, while heading the noon King's Cross-Edinburgh service.

Travelling at around 50mph just south of Thirsk, the driver realised to his horror that a northbound block cement train on an adjacent line had derailed. Although most of the wagons were clear of the main line, one was foul, and the locomotive struck it on the driver's side. As the passenger train passed along the derailed freight, extensive damage was caused to most vehicles. Seven passengers were killed and 45 injured. The Thirsk signalman averted further disaster by throwing all his signals to danger and sending an obstruction danger bell code to the Northallerton and Pilmoor boxes either side, stopping a London-bound express at Thirsk station less than five miles to the north. Had he not done so, this express would have struck the wreckage only a few minutes later. D283, the English Electric Type 4 diesel hauling the goods train, was undamaged.

The BR Research Division at Derby investigated the accident, and Colonel D. McMullen chaired a formal inquiry. The cause of the derailment of the block cement train was its instability at its maximum speed, 45mph. The suspension type fitted to the wagons was based on a continental design and the presence of cement dust, acting as an abrasive on the suspension, caused excessive wear, which under test conditions showed the vehicle type to be outside the safe margins of movement at speeds above 35mph. Two possible contributing factors to the derailment were wear on the wheel flanges and minor track irregularities.

After the accident, a speed restriction of 35mph was placed on loaded CemFlo wagons and 50mph unloaded on other wagons of the same type, and modifications to the vehicles' coupling and buffering arrangements were enacted. DP2, which was still owned by the English Electric Company, and operating along with the Deltic fleet on East Coast Main Line expresses at the time of the derailment, was moved to York traction and maintenance depot and eventually back to its Vulcan Foundry birthplace. The decision was taken not to effect repairs, and it was broken up in 1968 – but its engine and other parts lived on. They were given to the Class 50 diesel pool of spares, and the engine initially went to D417/50017 *Royal Oak*, but ended its working days in No. 50037.

———————————— *Chapter 21* ————————————

1967 HITHER GREEN: BONFIRE NIGHT HORROR

A broken rail caused the derailment of a run-of-the-mill electric service at Hither Green in London on November 5, 1967, leaving 49 people dead and 78 people injured. The accident speeded up plans to replace fishplates and traditional rail joints with continuous welded rail. That Sunday, the 12-coach 7.43pm Hastings to Charing Cross service, formed by six-car DEMUs Nos. 1007 (Class 201 or 6S) leading 1017 (Class 202 or 6L) – and travelling at around 70mph – derailed at 9.16pm. The derailment occurred just before the St Mildred's Road railway bridge between Hither Green and Grove Park stations near the Southern Region Continental goods depot. The leading pair of wheels on the third coach were derailed by a broken rail and ran on for a quarter of a mile before striking points, causing 11 coaches to be derailed, four of which turned on to their sides. The train came to rest after 250 yards, apart from the leading coach; it detached and ran on for a further 220 yards.

Forty-nine passengers were killed and 78 injured, 27 being detained in hospital. Most of the casualties had been travelling in the overturned coaches. The driver and guard escaped unharmed, but remained in a state of shock. Emergency services arrived within five minutes and the first casualty arrived at hospital 18 minutes after the derailment. Local residents, the Salvation Army and the Women's Voluntary Service assisted the injured.

A British Pathé newsreel shows the smashed and twisted wreckage and rescuers using a rope in a bid to right a carriage. Fire crews, who were working under floodlights, were also seen crawling through the remains in an attempt to find survivors and using special equipment to cut through the coaches to release passengers. Driving rain and the position of some of the overturned coaches made the rescue operation especially difficult. Doctors also had to crawl through twisted wreckage to treat survivors and give them painkilling injections. Most of the survivors were taken to Lewisham Hospital, praised for its work after the Lewisham train disaster, which had occurred just a mile away 10 years before. The last survivor was taken to hospital at 1am the next day.

The fast lines were blocked by the derailment and the traction current to the slow lines was switched off to allow the rescue. Power was temporarily restored to the slow lines for the Tuesday morning rush hour and returned to traffic that afternoon. The fast lines were reopened with a speed restriction at 6.20am on the Wednesday. The subsequent investigation found that the accident had been caused by a broken rail at a rail joint. A fatigue crack through the first bolt-hole in a running-on rail had progressively developed and a triangular piece of rail had broken out. The sleeper at the joint had previously failed and been replaced with a shallower timber replacement. This replacement had not been well packed, was on a shallow layer of clean ballast and the rubber pad supporting the rail on the adjacent concrete sleeper was missing. The accident sparked questions about trains running at excessive speed. The speed limit for EMUs on the track had been raised from 75mph to 90mph in July that year.

THE BEE GEE WHO WAS STAYIN' ALIVE

Among the survivors were 17-year-old singer Robin Gibb of the Bee Gees and his wife-to-be Molly Hullis. Claiming that travelling in a first-class coach – which he could afford after the band had just had a smash UK hit with *Massachusetts* – may have saved his life. Gibb recalled the horror in an interview only four months before his death in May 2012 at the age of 62. He told the *Mail on Sunday*: "My fiancee Molly – later my first wife – and I were travelling on a train from Hastings to London and, thanks to *Massachusetts*, I could afford a first-class compartment. That might well have saved us. I'd flown in from Berlin early that morning, and as we boarded the train, Molly remarked that with all my flying around, I ought to get some travel insurance. An irony, given what was about to happen. Then we settled back in our seats, facing each other, me in a mac and trilby, and Molly in a green-and-white coat with a fur collar. Soon after we had passed Lewisham, I heard what sounded like rocks hitting the train. I looked round in alarm and said to Molly: 'This train is going to crash!' She didn't believe me because, as her mother lived in Hastings, she'd taken the same train journey every week for years without mishap. But I knew I was right, so I reached up for the emergency cord. Before I could pull it, the lights went out.

"I didn't know it at the time, but we were hurtling along at 90mph. Our carriage tilted to one side and then broken glass flew all over us like Niagara Falls. I had long hair, and the glass got tangled in it. It took me days afterwards to remove the shards. Then a piece of steel railway line shot through a window and passed my face. If I had been standing an inch forward, I would have been decapitated. If we hadn't been sitting in first class in the front of the train, but in a second-class carriage in the middle of the train (the part of the train that jack-knifed), the impact on us would have been even more devastating. There is a high chance that we would have been killed or seriously injured. The train came to rest. Our carriage was separated from the others. Molly and I looked out of the broken window, and all we could see were silhouettes of all the other carriages – upside down, sideways, in the embankment, in the road.

"Molly and I were covered in oil but otherwise unhurt. All around us people were screaming and moaning. We managed to climb out of a window and I helped other people out of their compartments. I did the best I could. One little old lady refused, though. She was holding on to her ticket and told me she wasn't getting off the train yet as her ticket was to Charing Cross. The rescue services had to get her out. Eventually, we got up on to a bridge above the track. Through it all, the Bonfire Night fireworks were flaring all around us. We were taken to a hospital in Lewisham so they could examine us. When we arrived there, the scene was like something out of a war zone. All around us, people on stretchers were being carried in. Some of the injuries were horrific. I'd written about terrible events on a previous occasion; the Bee Gees' *New York Mining Disaster 1941* was inspired by the Aberfan disaster (when a collapsing slag heap crushed the primary school in the Welsh village in 1966). But I couldn't write about Hither Green because I couldn't bear to think about it. Nor do I ever dream about it. I have seen the terrible fragility of human life."

Shirley Ward, a 21-year-old secretary from Broadstairs who emerged unharmed from the wreckage, told *The Times*: "The lights went out before we turned over. We felt ourselves travelling along on the carriage's side. Everyone was clutching on to one another. There were some terrible screams." Another survivor, Ray Moore, 19, a medical student from Hastings, said: "Stones came chipping up from the track as we went along this stretch, which is usually a pretty fast one. Then it rocked and swayed and went over on its side. At least three people in my compartment were killed."

Henrietta Baynes, 21, of Seal, near Sevenoaks, who at the time worked in the lingerie department of Fortnum and Mason, said: "The carriage started jolting violently as if we were riding on a bumpy road. The next thing I knew was that the carriage had been thrown over and I found myself on top of three or four other people. I was praying as it happened. Windows were shattered and the lights had gone out. People were hysterical but I found myself surprisingly calm and I helped other people. A porter came crawling along the luggage rack and asked if the door could be opened. It slid open and we all crawled out. There were people lying everywhere and there was one man trapped between the carriage and the track. We stood shivering at the side and then we were carried over the live electric rail." She found a £5 note on the track, equivalent to a week's wage, and was told to keep it. A newspaper reporter helped her up the steep bank and then drove her to London.

CONTINUOUS WELDED RAIL THE WAY AHEAD

After the derailment, the line was inspected and a temporary speed restriction of 60mph imposed. Complaints were also received about the rough riding of Hastings line stock. Another DEMU of the same class was tested on Southern Region and Eastern Region lines. Although the ride quality was better on the Eastern Region track, it was not considered dangerous on Southern Region track. The Ministry of Transport report into the accident criticised the maintenance of the line, especially following a recent increase of the maximum speed of trains over the route. Colonel D. McMullen's report found that civil engineering and inspection departments had not only permitted too low a standard of maintenance on the line but failed to assess the implications of increasing the speed of the trains.

In his conclusion he said: "The rail fracture was the result of the unsatisfactory support condition of the joint; the fracture could not reasonably have been foreseen and I hold no-one responsible for it. Many steps have been and are being taken to prevent rail joints being in such an unsatisfactory support condition. These steps and the more frequent testing of rails should considerably reduce the chances of rail fractures in existing track, but fractures will never be completely eliminated. Additional steps have been and are being taken that should also reduce considerably the chances of rail fractures in new track. The general standard of maintenance of the section on which the derailment occurred was inadequate for the speed at which trains were being run. I attach responsibility for this to the permanent way staff, the chief permanent way inspector, the district engineer and the chief civil engineer. All possible steps are being taken to improve the standard of maintenance generally on the Southern Region, but this will be a long process. I recommend that in main lines and heavily trafficked commuter lines the premature replacement of jointed track by continuous welded rail should be speeded-up to the maximum practical extent." So maintenance of the line was improved, inspection techniques and jointing methods were revised, and, more significantly, plans for replacing jointed track by continuous welded rail were accelerated. Concrete sleepers were banned at rail joints on the Southern Region.

Chapter 22

1975 MOORGATE: SO WHY DIDN'T HE STOP?

In the worst peacetime accident in the history of London Underground, nobody ever established beyond doubt why Northern Line driver Leslie Newson failed to stop before his tube train crashed into a wall at the Moorgate terminus killing 43 people. At 8.46am in the rush hour of February 28, 1975, a Northern City Line tube train comprising two three-car sets of 1938 stock and carrying around 300 people appeared to accelerate as it approached the terminus of the Highbury branch at Moorgate. Passengers waiting on the platform noticed the vacant stare on the 56-year-old driver Leslie Newson's face as his train hurtled past the platforms at up to 40mph. Seconds later, the tube train entered the 66ft overrun tunnel, which was equipped with a red stop-lamp, a sand drag and hydraulic buffer stop. The sand drag slowed the train only slightly before it impacted on the buffer stops and then the wall behind them, killing 43 people and injuring another 74.

Two minutes after the impact, emergency services were called and the first ambulances were on the scene at 8.54am followed by the fire brigade at 8.58am. The Post Office set up emergency telephone lines in the station for the rescuers. Survivor Javier Gonzalez told the BBC: "Just above my newspaper I saw a lady sitting opposite me and then the lights went out. I have the image of her face to this day. She died. As darkness came, there was a very loud noise of the crash, metal and glass breaking, no screams, all in the fraction of a second one takes to breathe in. It was all over in no time. I had been knocked unconscious and have no further memory until I heard a shout in the distance: 'Is there anybody else there?' And there was complete silence. Then my preservation instinct made me shout back: 'Yes, I am here!'" He was taken to St Bartholomew's hospital where he spent several weeks recovering from his injuries. It took 13 hours to free the last survivor, and the final body to be recovered was that of the driver more than four days later.

Normal full services did not resume until 10 days after the crash. The Department of the Environment report on the disaster was published on March 4. It stated that no fault had been found with the train during tests, while there was evidence that the driver's hand was on the 'dead man's handle', rather than in front of his face to protect himself – suggesting that he had made no effort to stop. Several of the train's passengers said that it had speeded up rather than slowed down when entering Moorgate. Platform witnesses said that driver Newson was sitting upright in his seat and looking straight ahead as the train sped past. Two railwaymen waiting on Platform 9 recognised the driver sitting bolt upright in his cabin, with his hands on the controls and staring straight ahead. "He made no attempt to move as we flung ourselves against the platform wall, instinctively throwing up our arms to protect our heads," one of the men said later. Experts ascertained that power had been applied to the train's motors until within two seconds of the impact.

MOORGATE'S UNSOLVED MYSTERY

So what went wrong? Why did driver Newson not react? That question is still being asked today. He had worked for the Underground since 1969. A post-mortem examination did not find any evidence of an incapacitating medical problem such as stroke or a heart attack. Analysis at the post-mortem showed that the level of alcohol level in his blood was 80 milligrams per 100 millilitres, the same as the limit for car drivers. However, a definite conclusion could not be reached as to whether this level was the result of drinking or the process of decomposition, as it had taken so long to recover the body. Evidence to the official inquiry raised the possibility that the driver had been affected by a condition such as transient global amnesia or akinesis with mutism, where the brain continues to function and the individual remains aware, although not being able to move. Yet there was no evidence to indicate either condition. Driver Newson had £270 in his pocket, which he was hoping to use to buy a car for his daughter when his shift ended. If he had taken the trouble of getting the money out of the bank or other place of safekeeping, why would he then have taken his own life?

City of London coroner, Dr. David Paul, returned a verdict of accidental death, and a Department of the Environment report found that there was insufficient evidence to say if the accident was down to a deliberate act or a medical condition. By pure coincidence, *Sunday Times* reporter Laurence Marks was sent to cover the crash on that dreadful day – after making hourly calls to the police emergency helpline for relatives of victims, fearing that his 68-year-old father might be a passenger. Yet at the time, there was no record of a Bernard Marks on the casualty lists. Laurence went home, but did not sleep, his mind gripped with fear. At 11am the next day, a police constable knocked at the door of his home, came in and sat down, and said that the body of his father had been removed from the wreckage at 4.30am.

Laurence Marks spent nearly a year investigating the crash, and spoke to numerous witnesses and people involved, from the coroner to the driver's widow and daughters. He presented a Channel 4 documentary, *Me, My Dad and Moorgate*, broadcast on June 4, 2006, expressing his by then long-held personal belief that the crash was suicide. Looking in detail at the inquest report, he unearthed a claim that the driver had overshot a terminal platform by a carriage length a week before – highly unusual for a well-respected railwayman who was known to be meticulous. It was hypothesised that the driver might have lost concentration, or become confused by the similar design of the stations, in a 2009 episode of BBC Radio 4's *In Living Memory*.

NEW SAFETY SYSTEM INSTALLED AFTER CRASH
Following the crash, a safety system that stops a train automatically if the driver fails to brake was introduced on the Tube. Since the death of a driver in 1971, when an empty tube stock train failed to stop in tunnel sidings, London Underground had been introducing speed controls at such locations. By the time of the Moorgate crash, 12 out of the 13 locations had the equipment in place. Shortly after the crash, London Underground changed the operating instructions, so that the protecting signal at terminal platforms was held at danger until trains approaching were travelling slowly, or had been brought to a stop, only to find that this practice produced delays and operating problems.

In July 1978, TETS (Trains Entering Terminal Stations), colloquially known as Moorgate Protection and Moorgate Control after the collision, was approved for installation at all dead-end termini on manually driven lines on the Underground. The normal stopping position for a train has a signal fixed at danger and improved arrestors are placed beyond this point. Timing relays ensure that trains enter stations at low speeds. Resistors are also placed in the traction supply, to stop a train accelerating when entering the platforms. The system was operational in all locations by 1984. Totally unconnected with the crash, Underground services into Moorgate on the Northern City Line had already been scheduled to be replaced by British Rail services from Welwyn Garden City and Hertford. The final tube services ran into Moorgate on October 4, 1975 and BR services began in August 1976, having previously terminated at Broad Street station.

Chapter 23

1975 NUNEATON: NIGHTMARE AFTER SIGNALS MISSED

S ix people lost their lives and another 38 were injured south of Nuneaton shortly before 2am on June 6, 1975, when a sleeper train ran too fast through a temporary 20mph speed restriction. The 11.30pm West Coast Main Line overnight sleeper service from Euston to Glasgow comprising Class 86 electric locomotives Nos. 86006 and 86242 and 15 carriages, including 12 sleeping cars, was behind schedule. A locomotive failure further south meant that it was running more than one hour late, and the experienced driver, J. McKay, tried to make up for lost time. Signal boxes were clear and the train was travelling safely at its authorised speed. But approaching the station around 1.55am, at Nuneaton it all changed. The driver failed to remember instructions he had been given about a temporary speed limit of 20mph on one section because of a track-remodelling scheme.

More than a mile before the restriction, there was a board giving advance warning of the restriction. It was of standard design – a horizontal arrow with two 'bullseye' lights and, above it, a black square panel, also lit, showing a white '20'. It should have been illuminated, but was not. Driver McKay claimed that he wrongly assumed that this meant the restriction had been lifted, and so did not slow the train. The board marking the actual start of the restriction, however, was lit, but by the time he saw this, it was too late. Despite an emergency brake application, the train entered the 20mph restriction at around 70mph and became derailed on a length of temporary track being used during the remodelling scheme. The 86s became detached from each another, the second mounting the northbound platform and causing damage to the station. The coaches slewed sideways for a distance of 340 yards and the front carriage finally came to rest with its front end on top of the platform and in contact with the platform awning. While the first two carriages stayed mainly upright, the next four fell on to their sides and were badly crushed.

Six people (four passengers and two sleeping car attendants) in these four sleeping cars died. Another 38 on board the train were injured and taken to Manor Hospital in Nuneaton. Phil Williams, who was among the first fire crews on the scene, remembered: "There was one locomotive up on the platform and then, as we looked along the track, carriages were scattered all over the place. People were spilling out, injured and in shock. The scale of it was beyond my experience. Some parts of the train were crumpled, like crushed cigarette packets or squashed tin cans, and the middle section had telescoped. The overhead power lines were down and we got hose reels out in case of fire." Fire crews used ladders to access the roofs of the overturned carriages so that trapped casualties could be reached. Many of the passengers were in their beds, under blankets, when the crash happened, helping to reduce the casualty list. It was 7.39am before the last injured person could be released from the wreckage. The last body was not removed until 5.28pm and the search of the wreckage continued until 11.45pm the following day.

DRIVER CLEARED OF ALL BLAME
Every coach on the train was derailed except the last, and more than a quarter of a mile

of track was destroyed along with three lineside electrification gantries. Severe damage was caused to an overhead road bridge, numerous other items of trackside equipment, and Class 25 diesel No. 25286, which was hauling a passing freight train. The casualties would have been much higher if not for the fact there were fewer than 100 passengers on board. The inquiry, conducted by Major C.F. Rose, highlighted three causes for the disaster. First, the gas equipment, which powered the warning lights on the advance warning board, was not being used properly, and had gone out. Secondly, several drivers on earlier trains had seen that the lights had gone out, yet did not stop at Nuneaton to report it. Thirdly, Major Rose said that although he denied it had been the case, it was thought likely that the driver, in his haste to make up lost time, forgot about the speed restriction without the reminder of the advance warning board. He concluded his report by stating: "I am pleased to report that the Railways Board has decided in principle to install AWS (the Automatic Warning System) permanent magnets in association with warning boards on the approach to temporary speed restrictions on lines where AWS is provided. Priority will be given to the high-speed inter-city lines."

Driver McKay, 36, who was based at Euston, had been a railwayman for 20 years and had qualified as a driver in 1967. He had thus had many years' experience on the West Coast Main Line and was very familiar with the lines between Rugby and Nuneaton. On May 24, McKay received and signed for the notice of temporary speed restrictions, and permanent way operations covering the period from then to Friday, June 6. He appeared at Birmingham Crown Court on June 9, 1976 to answer six charges of manslaughter. After a three-day trial he was found not guilty and discharged. However, multiple recommendations to prevent a recurrence of the accident were accepted by the British Railways Board. Furthermore, the later installation of the Automatic Warning System ensured that drivers were given audible notice of speed restrictions. Both locomotives in the crash were rebuilt and re-entered traffic. No. 86242, which ended up buried in Nuneaton station canopy, was in 2013 sold to a private railway company, FLOYD, in Hungary being renumbered 450 008.

On August 8, 2015, crowds gathered at the station for the unveiling by the Mayor of Nuneaton and Bedworth, Councillor Barry Longden, and Nuneaton MP Marcus Jones of a memorial to honour those who lost their lives in the disaster 40 years before. They were joined by Paul Gough, town crier for Nuneaton and Bedworth, Carole Williams, town crier for Bishop's Stortford, Rev. Kelly Betteridge, vicar of St Nicolas Parish Church, the Burbage Silver Band and Patrick Verwer, managing director of London Midland. The memorial was the idea of Nuneaton Memories, founded by Mark Palmer, who raised funds for the plaque, and was supported by donations from local people and ex-Nuneatonians across the world.

Chapter 24

1988 CLAPHAM JUNCTION: THE
WRONG KIND OF WIRE

An errant wire led to the deaths of 35 people in a collision at Clapham Junction, the busiest place on the UK rail network, during the early rush hour of Monday, December 12, 1988. However, the principal cause was the fact that a British Rail signalling technician had not had a day off in 13 weeks.

That morning, the usual procession of Up commuter trains were making their way towards Clapham Junction en route to Waterloo along the four-track route. On the fast line, the driver of the crowded 7.18am from Basingstoke, comprising three four-car 4VEP electric multiple units, suddenly saw signal WF138 change from green to red about 30 yards ahead of him. Although he made an emergency brake application, he overran it but realised that he would not stop far short of the next signal along the line (WF47). He accordingly continued to that point and used its telephone to report the Signal Passed At Danger. He had every right to assume that WF138 would be showing red behind him to protect his train. The sudden change of aspect of WF138, however, had been down to a rogue wire that had been left in the relay room at Clapham Junction following re-signalling work carried out on the two previous Sundays as part of the Waterloo Area Re-signalling Scheme. New wiring had been needed between a fuse and a relay and this had been installed on the first weekend, but contrary to instructions, the old wire had been severed only at the relay (bottom) end, the rest of the surrounding equipment keeping it clear of the terminal to which it had been attached.

On the second Sunday, however, sufficient other changes had been made for the rogue wire, left connected at one end, and loose and uninsulated at the other, to be able to 'remember' its original position and make contact with the relay. As a result, power reached the relay and made the signal show green even when the track circuit ahead was occupied. While the driver of the Basingstoke train was reporting the incident by telephone, the following train, the 6.30am from Bournemouth made up of a 4REP and two 4TC multiple units running under clear signals, came round the curve, where the driver suddenly saw the rear of the train in front. Despite immediate emergency braking, the two collided, some of the wreckage fouling the adjacent Down fast line, where it was hit by an empty stock train comprising two four-car 4VEP units. Eight of the 20 cars overturned and three were hurled into the air. Ronald Arlette, 52, who was on the Basingstoke train, said: "There was an almighty bang, like an explosion. The carriage went up and we flew over and over."

The driver of the Basingstoke train was standing by the telephone when his train was pushed forward several feet by the collision. He picked up the receiver and spoke to the signalman, informing him of the collision and asking him to call the emergency services. The signalman immediately switched all the signals he could to danger, and signalled to the adjacent signal boxes that he had an obstruction on the line. However, he had no control over automatic signals, and was not able to stop a fourth train. Fortunately, the driver of this train, who got a yellow at WF138, saw the wreckage ahead and stopped behind the other two and the signal that should have protected them, which was showing a yellow caution aspect instead of a red danger aspect. The signalman then called the Clapham Junction station manager and asked him to call the emergency services. The accident had tripped the high-voltage feed to the traction current. The operator in the electrical control suspected there had been a derailment and reconfigured the supply so that the nearby Wimbledon line trains could still run. The collision claimed the lives of 33 people while 69 were seriously injured and another 415 received minor injuries. Two more died later.

Pupils and teachers from the nearby Emanuel School were first on the scene of the disaster and did what they could to offer assistance. Prime Minister Margaret Thatcher, who visited the victims in hospital, later commended them for their response. As the accident was in central London, members of the public made the first 999 calls. The fire brigade arrived at 8.17am and ambulances at 8.21am. By 8.27am, a major incident had been declared. The Metropolitan Police used its helicopter to fly doctors to the site. Rescue attempts were hampered because the railway was in a cutting, with a metal fence at the top and a wall at the bottom of a wooded slope. Council workers cut away the fence, trees and shrubs on the slope, into which steps were cut. A mobile canteen was organised by the Salvation Army. Survivors needed to be cut out of the tangled carriages before being transferred to St George's Hospital in Tooting, although some were so badly injured that they required emergency procedures at the scene. The last casualty was taken to hospital at 1.04pm and the last body was removed at 3.45pm.

THE 56-DAY PUBLIC INQUIRY

The Basingstoke train had stopped at the next signal after the faulty signal, in accordance with the rule book. If the Basingstoke train had carried on to the next signal, then the crash would not have happened, because it would have been protected by a working track circuit. Four days after the crash, British Rail admitted responsibility for the signalling wire fault. A full public inquiry for the Department for Transport was conducted into the crash by Sir Anthony Hidden QC and sat for 56 days from January to May 1989. He found that the signalling technician responsible had not been told his working practices were wrong and that an independent person had not inspected his work. He had also worked a seven-day week for the previous 13 weeks.

A 1978 British Rail Southern Region report had concluded that owing to the age of the equipment, the re-signalling was needed by 1986; approval was given in 1984 after a report of three wrong-side signal failures. The re-signalling project had been planned assuming more people were available, and employees felt that the programme was inflexible and felt under pressure to get the work done. Installation and testing were carried out at weekends during voluntary overtime. The signalling technician who had done the work had not cut back, insulated or tied back the loose wire and his work had not been supervised, nor had his work been inspected by an independent person as was required. A wire count that would have identified that a wire had not been removed was not carried out.

Hidden found that there had been inadequate training, assessment, supervision, testing, or effective monitoring. Critical of the Health and Safety culture within British Rail at the time, Hidden's 230-page report contained no fewer than 93 recommendations; it was sent to the Secretary of State nine months later. Hidden recommended that unused signal wires needed to be cut back and insulated, and that a testing plan be in place, with the inspection and testing being done by an independent person. Signal technicians needed to attend refresher courses every five years, and testers needed to be trained and certified, he said. Management were to ensure that no one was working high levels of overtime, and a senior project manager should be made responsible for all aspects of the project. Unprotected wrong-side signal failures – where the failure permitted a train to go beyond where it was permitted – had to be reported to HM Railway Inspectorate, he said. Cab radios, linking driver and signalman, were recommended, along with the installation of public address systems on existing trains that were not scheduled to be withdrawn within five years.

Hidden also made the recommendation that automatic train protection, which was being considered by BR at that time, should be implemented fully by 1996-97 – despite the fact that even if it had been installed at Clapham in December 1988, it would have similarly given a faulty indication and so would not have prevented the collision. When the expenditure needed to install automatic train protection had been fully assessed, it became apparent that the cost per likely life saved was extremely high, and so successive governments shied away from providing the money for its widespread installation. However, other simpler protection schemes, such as the cheaper Train Protection & Warning System, have since been developed to fulfil the same function as automatic train protection.

FINED £250,000 – BUT THE PUBLIC PAYS

In June 1991 the British Railways Board appeared before Judge Wright at the Central Criminal Court and pleaded guilty to two charges concerning its failure to ensure the health and safety of passengers and employees. The judge described the collision as, "one of the most grievous train disasters of recent years, certainly in this country." Adding: "The immediate cause of the signalling failure, which led to the situation in the Clapham area on the morning of the accident, was the failure to observe basic rules of electrical engineering practice by an individual technician. That failure was able to occur, and to go uncorrected, in the context of a series of system failures in the signals and telecommunications department of the Southern Region of British Rail, which went to the very top of the organisation.

"It is entirely clear from the evidence that is before me that there was a failure of any proper system of preparation for work, supervision of work, inspection of work, testing and checking of work of the re-signalling work that was being carried out at the material time in the Waterloo area. Standing instructions were not properly distributed; individual personnel were not fully trained or instructed in their responsibilities; there was no proper co-ordination of instructions or system for ensuring that these instructions were complied with. The level to which these standards had fallen is illustrated by the fact that there were two other incidents, fortunately causing no accident: one at Oxted in November 1985, and one at Queen's Road, Battersea, in June 1988.

"The accident of December 12, 1988 occurred because these defendants, the British Railways Board, allowed those standards to fall below any acceptable level. The result was a state of affairs in the railway cuttings between Earlsfield and Clapham Junction stations on that morning of quite horrifying danger." He continued: "In cases of this kind – and I do not wish to be misunderstood when I say this – penalty is not usually of major importance or the greatest importance. The real impact of a prosecution under the Health and Safety at Work Act, especially in the case of a major public undertaking, is the disgrace; the disgrace of being publicly condemned before a criminal court."

He then questioned exactly who would be punished by the £250,000 fine that he was about to impose. "In the case of a public authority that is funded either by the taxpayer or, as here, by a combination of the taxpayer and the fare-paying public, the question of penalty raises an acute problem. A swingeing fine of the magnitude that some, even now, might consider appropriate in the circumstances of this case, could only be met by the Board either by increasing the burden on the fare-paying passengers – which is hardly logical, having regard to the fact that it is for the benefit of the fare-paying passengers that this legislation exists – or by reducing the funds available for improvements in the railway system in general. That, again, could hardly be regarded as a desirable state of affairs. On the other hand, I must bear in mind the necessity of marking the disapproval of society at the failures demonstrated by those charged with British Rail management at the material time leading up to, and causing, this accident. An insignificant fine would rightly, in my judgment, bring down upon myself, and upon the whole system of justice, universal condemnation. I, therefore, have to steer a narrow course between these two alternative hazards." The British Railways Board was also ordered to pay £55,000 costs.

In the wake of the crash, testing on British Rail signalling work was made mandatory and the working hours of employees involved in safety-critical work was limited. Furthermore, although British Rail was fined, there was anger that there was no prosecution for manslaughter. The collision was one of the events cited in 1996 by the Law Commission as a reason for the new law on manslaughter, resulting in the Corporate Manslaughter and Corporate Homicide Act 2007.

REMEMBERING A QUARTER OF A CENTURY ON
A memorial marking the location of the crash site stands on top of the embankment above the railway in Spencer Park Green, Battersea. An outdoor memorial service took place there 10 years after the disaster, attended by more than 200 people. At 8.13am on December 12, 2013, a two-minute silence was held to remember the 35 people who died in the crash that same moment 25 years before. Survivors again attended a service at the crash memorial site, and a second service was attended by train drivers and representatives of their union, ASLEF. Prayers at the service mentioned the pupils of nearby Emanuel School, who helped treat the injured. Before the service, rail minister, Baroness Kramer, paid tribute to those who had lost their lives. "Important lessons have been learnt since then and Britain today has one of the safest rail networks in the world," she said. "However, we must never become complacent. We must always make sure that safety remains the number one priority on our railways."

Chapter 25

1994 COWDEN – SO, WHO WAS DRIVING?

Branch lines are not normally noted for serious accidents, but on October 15, 1988, five people lost their lives in a head-on crash in thick fog 400 yards south-east of Cowden station in Kent on the Uckfield branch. The collision occurred after the driver of a northbound train ran past a red signal and entered the single-line section. It should have passed a southbound train at Ashurst, but late running meant that didn't happen. The two six-car Class 205 diesel multiple units involved in the disaster were not travelling particularly fast and their combined speed was 65mph. However, that was enough to destroy both the leading vehicles and throw the driving coach of the southbound train down an embankment. The impact was so severe that it was two days before the body of the final victim could be removed. Both drivers and the guard of the Up train and two passengers, a couple from Crowborough travelling in the leading coach of the northbound train, were killed, and 11 people were injured.

In his subsequent inquiry report, Assistant Chief Inspecting Officer of Railways Major Kit Holden ruled that the driver of the Up train passing the protecting signal between Ashurst and Blackham Junction at danger had caused the collision. There had been poor visibility but there was no evidence of equipment failure. Although the Oxted signalman was aware that a collision would ensue, he was powerless to act as no box-to-train telephone system had been installed. A lengthy part of the report dealt with the question of who was actually driving the Up train. The guard, Jonathan Brett-Andrews, 36, a train enthusiast who had failed his drivers' examination and been reprimanded twice for driving trains, had previously been cautioned for riding in cabs… and the position of his body proved he had indeed been doing so on the day in question. However, because he and both drivers were killed in the collision and the front ends of both trains were so badly damaged, Home Office pathology examinations were unable to ascertain the exact positions of the crew in the northbound train at the point of impact. Both were found pinned between the roof of their driving trailer and the front of the other train.

Major Holden stated in his report that the guard had been an unnecessary distraction to the 31-year-old driver, Brian Barton. The question of base-to-train communication equipment was also addressed. Major Holden said the accident might not have happened if two-way radios had been fitted in the trains. A signalman had noticed that Mr Barton's train had tripped the points but was unable to alert the drivers because the trains did not have radios. David Rees, the driver of the southbound train, was absolved of all responsibility for the accident. At the subsequent inquest in Tunbridge Wells, Kent, accidental death verdicts were returned on Mr Barton and Mr Brett-Andrews, while open verdicts were returned on the other three crash victims. Coroner Frank Warriner said that there was no evidence to prove exactly what had happened. "Whoever was driving, why did he not stop at the signals? I fear that question will never be answered satisfactorily." While the front vehicles of each train were cut up at the scene, four of the carriages survived into preservation.

In his report, Major Holden called for a detailed research programme into incidents of signals passed at danger. Six years later, and as a result of the Ladbroke Grove disaster, as described in Chapter 28, such a report was finally issued.

Chapter 26

1996 RICKERSCOTE: QUESTIONS OVER WAGON MAINTENANCE

A fatal crash, which left a locomotive in the front garden of a private house at Rickerscote near Stafford on March 8, 1996, led to a streamlining of wagon safety standards throughout the network.

That Friday, the 9.40pm Coventry to Glasgow Travelling Post Office train hauled by Rail Express Systems Class 86 electric locomotive No. 86239 collided with a Mossend-Bescot freight train that had derailed on the adjacent track at Rickerscote, just south of Stafford on the West Coast Main Line. The freight train had just passed Stafford's Trent Valley Junction when the leading axle of the ninth wagon in its 23-wagon consist failed, derailing the vehicle. One axle of the wagon, a tanker containing liquid carbon dioxide, sustained a complete fracture. The force of the derailment split the couplings, leaving the four-wheeled chemical tank wagon and a number of the following vehicles fouling the path of the TPO mail train, which was travelling at 60mph. The driver of the train realised that his formation had become parted when the air brakes began to bring his double-headed locomotives and remaining payload to a halt. However, before he had time to respond, he saw the TPO hauled by Class 86 No. 86239 pass him in the opposite direction.

Graham Massey, the Crewe-based driver of the mail train, had no time to brake and the force of the collision spun the locomotive around and catapulted it up the embankment, where it came to rest in spectacular fashion just feet from the front door of a private house. The front four coaches of the TPO were totally derailed and piled up in concertina fashion behind the locomotive. Widower John Thomson, a Glasgow mail sorter working inside the TPO alongside his son, also John, of Barrmill, near Beith, Ayrshire, was killed in the crash and 22 others who had taken the full force of the impact, including the driver of the mail train, were injured to varying degrees. The driver escaped with a broken leg and fractured pelvis.

To exacerbate matters, several of the chemical tanks were split open in the crash, releasing carbon dioxide into the atmosphere and causing breathing difficulties for many of the Royal Mail and rescue staff. Fifty houses were evacuated as poisonous carbon dioxide gas escaped from seven of the 13 freight wagons. Investigators found that the condition of the track and signalling were satisfactory and did not contribute to the accident.

The HM Railway Inspectorate report issued that November found the cause of the axle fracture to be a crack caused by fatigue and likely to have been initiated by corrosion pitting on the axle's surface. This type of failure is a rare event given the thousands of axles in daily service under rail vehicles, the report said. However, previous similar failures were looked at as part of the investigation. The report found that the wagon that had developed the fault had travelled 69,000 miles since a previous safety test on its axles. By contrast, the recommended limit issued by British Rail Research was a test frequency of every 24,000 miles. During the investigation, it was discovered that wagons allowed to run on Railtrack were subject to different standards of maintenance, depending on who the owner/operator was. Since privatisation, stock owned by the new companies, including CAIB UK Ltd, which owned the freight wagons, at the time did not have to conform to the same uniform standards as the whole of the rail network did under British Rail.

In late January 2002, seven traumatised victims of the crash were awarded £832,500 in compensation at London's High Court. The biggest payout was to Hugh Crumlish from Ayrshire, who was awarded £405,000. Mr Crumlish was said to be so traumatised by the memory that he had to sit outside court as his barrister described the crash scene. Eight others had received a total of £112,925 compensation before the trial, after Railtrack and Derby-based Engineering Link Ltd. admitted liability for the accident, bringing the total damages to nearly £1 million. Gerwyn Samuel, counsel for the claimants, said at the hearing that the scene of "complete carnage" after the train crash would live in the victims' memories for the rest of their lives. He said every subsequent rail accident – including the Selby and Hatfield disasters – had "reawakened and exacerbated" the men's nightmares and flashbacks to the Rickerscote crash. Judge Mr Justice Mackay criticised Railtrack for waiting five years before admitting responsibility for the crash. The HMRI report recommended a harmonisation of standards for maintenance, design, and operation of railway vehicles throughout the rail industry, and charged Railtrack with the responsibility to bring the standards into line within three months, to eliminate safety risks.

—————————— *Chapter 27* ——————————

1997 SOUTHALL: BRITAIN'S TRAIN SAFETY SYSTEMS CONDEMNED

A Signal Passed At Danger (SPAD) at Southall on the approach to Paddington on September 19, 1997 led to the deaths of seven passengers in a two-train collision. In its wake, several recommendations were made, covering driver training and research into driver behaviour, crashworthiness and fleet maintenance, and not least of all, that old but vital chestnut of automatic train control systems.

That day, the Great Western Trains InterCity 125 High Speed Train service from Swansea to Paddington, with power cars Nos. 43173 and 43163, set off. The train, carrying 212 passengers, some of them journalists returning to the capital after the vote on Welsh devolution, would never reach its destination. The train's Automatic Warning System apparatus was defective, and it passed a red (danger) signal preceded by two cautionary signals. As the tracks straightened ahead of the HST, which was running at 125mph, driver Larry Harrison, who had been driving trains since 1975, saw an EWS Class 59, No. 59101, a mile ahead, moving "at a funny angle" with its train of 20 bogie hopper wagons. The freight train was coming out of London on the Down relief line, and was scheduled to cross Southall East Junction on its way into a goods yard south of the main lines. There, it was to collect 20 more wagons before travelling to the Mendip Quarries in Somerset to be loaded with limestone. Driver Harrison, to his utmost horror, realised that there was no way that he could stop his HST, even under full braking.

Class 59 driver Alan Bricker expected the approaching HST to stop, but was alarmed at its speed and brake application. He desperately tried to accelerate his train to get it out of its way, but it was too late. At 1.20pm, the front power car smashed into a 24-ton hopper wagon, and two seconds later Coach H hit another wagon. Still travelling at 60mph, the HST power car severed the brake pipes of the freight train, and the stranded rear hopper wagons came to an immediate halt. Coach H then smashed into a severed coupling from the freight train, and slid on to its left side. Coach G, the second in the HST formation, hit the back of the freight train, which had by then stopped. The hopper wagons were pushed back and jack-knifed, with the coach and the wagons it had struck lifting into the air. The coach then slid beneath the wagon, flattening its front. The back of the train then impacted with Coach G, which was bent into a half-curve shape. Coach F at the back of the HST derailed after hitting the freight train.

Six passengers were killed, and a seventh died in hospital. Five had been in Coach G and the other two in Coach H. Sixteen passengers were trapped under the wreckage and it took fire crews several hours to free them. The last of the bodies were removed from the mangled wreckage at 9.50pm. A total of 139 people were injured, many of them being taken to Central Middlesex Hospital, Ealing Hospital, Hillingdon Hospital and West Middlesex Hospital. One man with head and chest injuries was taken by air ambulance to the Royal London Hospital in Whitechapel. A blaze, which started leaking hydraulic fluid, was quickly extinguished by fire crews. "It's a miracle that more people were not killed – the close-up damage is unbelievable," said one rescue worker.

Deputy Prime Minister John Prescott arrived while the rescuers were still working, and demanded an urgent report. The collision would almost certainly have been avoided if the basic AWS equipment had been working. Although AWS is only an advisory system, it would have given the driver a clear audible warning that he would have had to acknowledge. At the time of the accident, the train's Automatic Train Protection was not switched on. Nor had it been required to do so, as there had been problems in service with the system. In any event, the driver was not trained how to use it. Driver Harrison voluntarily attended Southall police station to be interviewed about the accident, and was duly arrested. Earlier, the driver of the goods train was released after being questioned by detectives.

DRIVER ADMITTED THAT HE DID NOT SPOT WARNING SIGNALS
Giving evidence at the public inquiry into the disaster, chaired by Professor John Uff QC FREng, which began in the New Connaught Rooms in Holborn on September 20, 1999, Larry Harrison said that he had been packing a bag with rail documents just moments before the collision. He said he took, "five seconds or a little longer bending over to pack his bag while his train was speeding from Hayes to Southall." He denied taking his eyes off the track but admitted that he failed to see the pair of yellow warning signals. He then saw that his train was "whizzing" towards a red danger signal with the Class 59 crossing his path. He said: "I don't know how I missed the two cautionary signals. All I can say is that I was packing my bag. I pushed my body down to the left to reach the bag. When I saw the signal was red I applied the brakes. I noticed there was an engine at a funny angle. It was a Class 59 locomotive. It took me a few seconds, but then I realised there was going to be a collision."

He also said that he set off from Cardiff with a fault to the AWS, but explained that drivers were allowed to continue their journeys regardless and rely on their own sight to avoid potential dangers. He said: "I felt obliged to drive the train with the AWS isolated. I didn't want to get myself or my company in trouble." When asked, driver Harrison told the inquiry that as far as he was concerned, the responsibility for the accident lay with, "the train company which permitted the train to run with the AWS isolated." Larry Harrison denied accounts from witnesses who said that he had both feet resting on the dashboard while the HST was moving; he said that he may have had one leg resting on a raised ledge to stretch it and avoid getting cramp. He could not explain why he had missed the signals. A tape recording of him sobbing uncontrollably down a telephone line as he reported the accident at the side of the track was played at the inquiry. The driver apologised to the victims, and said that he had retired as a driver and would never drive a train again.

The first day of the inquiry saw live television coverage permitted for the first time, with cameras and radio recordings allowed on an unrestricted basis. In written evidence to the inquiry, Dr. Deborah Lucas, a senior psychologist at the Health and Safety Executive, stated that driver Harrison may have lapsed into a "micro-sleep" when he passed the signals at danger. She said that people can appear to be attentive with their eyes open and with "no loss of posture", but with much lower alertness. Professor John Groeger of Surrey University told the hearing that any experienced train driver would have "considerable difficulty" in operating for an extended period without the safety system active.

The inquiry heard that Larry Harrison had two blemishes on his record going back to the 1970s, each relating to signals passed at danger, although these both involved relatively low speed travel. "More significantly, an event occurred in December 1996 which was not formally reported as a driving offence, but a record was made," said Professor Uff in his report. "On this occasion, driver Harrison is recorded as having started a train without the proper signal from the guard shortly after an incident when driver Harrison's bag was misplaced. He was said to be flustered. Did the bag hold more significance than its contents might suggest? At least, this event showed that criticism of driver Harrison's conduct should not be lightly disregarded."

The action of the signalman in giving the freight train precedence over the HST with the faulty AWS was at first criticised – but he could not have known that the HST's AWS was not working, or that the driver would ignore the stop signals. The inquiry found the primary cause of the accident to be Larry Harrison's failure to respond to two signals warning him of the freight train on the track ahead. Professor Uff's subsequent report said that he may have "dozed off". The report into the accident said that drivers had become increasingly reliant on AWS with single-manning, and at high speeds, that it was no longer acceptable to run trains if such equipment was inoperative.

GREAT WESTERN TRAINS ON TRIAL
Larry Harrison, 52, from Greenford in Middlesex, was subsequently charged with manslaughter, but the case was dropped after the prosecution offered no evidence following legal submissions before the start of the trial at the Old Bailey in July 1999, and a not-guilty verdict was formally recorded. At the same pre-trial hearing, Great Western Trains was also found not guilty of manslaughter after the prosecution offered no evidence, after the company said it would plead guilty to the single charge of failing to provide transport to the public, "in such a way as to ensure that they were not exposed to risks to their health and safety." However, on July 27, 1999, GWT was fined what was then a record £1.5 million for "dereliction of duty" in not having a system to ensure that trains were not operated for long journeys with AWS inoperative.

Judge Mr Justice Scott Baker said that the public had the right to expect the highest standard of care from rail operators. "Great Western Trains failed to meet that standard and in my judgment they failed to meet it by a greater extent than they have been prepared to admit," he said. The judge said that the fine was not intended to, "nor can it, reflect the value of the lives lost or the injuries sustained in this disaster. It is, however, intended to reflect public concern at the offence." He said that the company should have turned the HST at Swansea to ensure that a locomotive was at the front with a working warning device. He criticised GWT's chief executive, Richard George, for not attending the three-day court hearing. "I am surprised that neither Mr George – who it is said is in personal charge of safety at GWT – nor any other director of the company came to court to express personally remorse for GWT's breach of the Health and Safety Act, and to allay any impression of complacency that may have been conveyed to the victims, their families and the public," he said. GWT representative, Knowles Mitchell, replied that Mr George – who had been a passenger on the train – did not attend court because he had been told he was not needed as a witness, but felt, "very deeply about what happened." Jenny Bacon, director general of the Health and Safety Executive, said: "This prosecution and record fine sends a vital message to the railway industry – safety must come first." However, Detective Superintendent Graham Satchell of the British Transport Police said: "You have to ask, how much impact will this fine have on a company with a turnover of hundreds of millions of pounds?"

The previous highest fine against a single company for a breach of the health and safety law was £1.2 million imposed on Balfour Beatty following the collapse of three tunnels during the building of the Heathrow rail link. However, Louise Christian, head of a steering group of solicitors handling claims for victims of the crash, described the fine as, "derisory and an insult," that, "will not hurt Great Western Trains in any way." Linda Rees, a magistrate from south Wales who survived the crash, said: "There must be a large element of deterrent in any punishment – but this fine is no deterrent at all. When you consider that the company paid £17 million to its shareholders last year, this fine is just a slap on the wrist." A spokesman for Great Western Trains, by then known as First Great Western, and nowadays Great Western Railway, said the company deeply regretted the loss of lives and injury caused by the tragedy. "While working within the rules, we have accepted there was a serious breach of the health and safety laws by failing to do all we reasonably could to avoid risk. We have adopted further measures so that what happened at Southall cannot occur again."

KEY RECOMMENDATIONS MADE
The main recommendations of the report into the Southall disaster were as follows. Firstly, GWT and Railtrack should consider extensions to the present coverage of ATP, and ATP should be maintained in fully operational state on GW lines currently fitted. AWS should be regarded as vital to the continued running of a train. Second, alignment and siting of signals should be checked at least annually. Railtrack should review the operation of automatic route setting to consider whether more green signals should be booked ahead of higher-speed trains. Third, consideration should be given to speeding up the earthing and isolation of traction current following an accident. Furthermore, safety briefings or other means of communicating safety information to passengers should be adopted. Also, a study should be carried out to determine whether freight wagons could be designed with less-aggressive features such as sharp edges, without detriment to their primary function.

The report called for the Association of Train Operating Companies to review ways in which internal safety features of coaches could be modified to provide the best means of emergency exit, including from vehicles lying on their sides. Another recommendation was that passenger representation at train crash inquiries should not be limited to those involved in the immediate accident. All trains to be fitted with 'black box' data recorders, it said. Failure to provide means of reporting faults was to be regarded as a disciplinary offence, and that simulators should be introduced for driver training, were two more measures. Following this accident and the subsequent Ladbroke Grove rail crash, as outlined in the next chapter, Train Operating Company First Great Western (the current name of Great Western Trains) required all its trains to have ATP switched on. If the equipment was found to be faulty, the train would be taken out of service.

——————— *Chapter 28* ———————

1999 LADBROKE GROVE: THE SIGNAL THAT COULD NOT BE SEEN

C omplaints that a signal on the busy tracks leading out of Paddington station could not be properly seen by train drivers were overlooked or ignored, until October 5, 1999, when 31 people died in a head-on collision between two trains at Ladbroke Grove which led to a raging inferno.

Around 8.06am, a three-car Thames Train Class 165 Turbo service left Paddington for Bedwyn in Wiltshire... a destination that it would never reach. Between Paddington and Ladbroke Grove Junction, about two miles away, the tracks were signalled to allow trains to run over them in either direction, in and out of the platforms of the Great Western's London terminus. West of Ladbroke Grove, the main line from London to South Wales and the west of England switched to the conventional layout of two lines in each direction carrying fast and slow trains. The Turbo train was due to have been routed onto the Down main line at Ladbroke Grove, and should have been held at a red signal there until this movement could be done safely. Instead, the train ran past the signal, and the points settings beyond this brought it 600 yards on to the Up main line. Around 8.09am as it was entering this line, it collided nearly head-on with the 6.03am First Great Western Class 125 High Speed Train from Cheltenham to Paddington, at a combined speed of about 130mph. The drivers of both trains involved were killed outright, as well as 29 others (24 on the Class 165, nine on the HST) as a result of the impact. The HST, which had a Class 43 power car at each end, and eight Mk.3 coaches, was far more substantial than the Class 165, the front carriage of which was totally destroyed.

The diesel fuel carried by this train was dispersed by the collision and ignited in a fireball, causing a series of separate fires in the wreckage, particularly in coach H at the front of the HST, which was completely burned out, with one further fatality as a result of the fire. A total of 227 people were admitted to hospital while a further 296 people were treated at the site of the crash for minor injuries. What surprised everyone about the crash, including experts, was the devastating fireball that spread so quickly. Why did it happen when diesel fuel would not normally behave in such a flammable manner?

Diesel will usually ignite only if it is turned into vapour by heat and reaches a temperature of 100-200°C – but in this case, both trains' fuel tanks contained a 'winter mix', in which the diesel was blended with a paraffin-like additive to act as an anti-coagulant and anti-waxing agent. Nevertheless, the additive quantities are understood to be small and should not have lowered the flashpoint so significantly. Several metallurgists suggested that the friction of steel on the HST rubbing against the aluminium of the Turbo unit would have created sufficient heat to ignite the spilt diesel. With fuel having poured through broken windows on to upholstery, it would not have been difficult for the fire to have taken hold once initial ignition had taken place. It appeared that parts of the aluminium Turbo train had melted. In addition to the main blaze in Coach H and the leading power car, fuel spillage caused a separate fire inside the Turbo's centre trailer car, which was just inches away from two of the HST's otherwise undamaged standard-class carriages. The towering column of black smoke that gutted Coach H was seen over a large area of west London. As we saw in Chapter 14, Britain's worst-ever railway disaster, Quintinshill, was also exacerbated by a fire in which many victims perished.

WHEN VICTIMS BECAME RESCUERS

A large number of passengers managed to get out of all of the vehicles except the obliterated leading Turbo coach – in which, miraculously, there were a handful of survivors. Despite suffering from lacerations and shock, many who had already escaped the wreckage desperately tried to go back to help those still trying to flee the flames. North Kensington fire station was just 300 yards from the crash site, and a well-rehearsed major incident plan swung into action. Yet fire crews took more than an hour to extinguish the inferno. Staff from a nearby Sainsbury's supermarket rallied round and turned their coffee shop into a casualty clearing station where paramedics dealt with the walking wounded. The Great Western Main Line, used by as many as 100,000 passengers a day, was closed completely after the crash, stranding two HST sets, four Heathrow Express units and at least five Turbo units in the platforms at Paddington, with all Great Western, Thames and Virgin Cross Country services terminated at Reading. The 63 more seriously injured, many of them suffering from 70-degree burns, broken limbs, internal injuries and the effects of smoke inhalation, were transferred to local hospitals, including St Mary's, next to Paddington station, whose staff had practised major incident procedures based on a rail crash.

Deputy Prime Minister and Transport Secretary John Prescott visited the scene within hours of the tragedy and later said he would consider resigning if there was another serious crash involving fatalities. Prime Minister Tony Blair braced the nation for a horrific death toll. National newspaper banner headlines speculated that as many as 170 people had died. Parts of the wreckage were buried 3ft deep in ash and debris, and identification of some of the other bodies was possible only by using dental records. However, the number of 'missing' passengers was gradually revised downwards. Police confirmed that some passengers had left the HST at Reading and flown abroad, unaware that they were listed as missing, while other 'missing' passengers turned out to be non-existent names created by sick hoax callers.

Ironically, the crash occurred while the public inquiry into the September 1997 Southall disaster was still being held, after having been delayed because of legal proceedings against the HST driver and his employer, Great Western Trains. Further media anger was stirred up when the re-use of the three Southall coaches became known. The Queen also visited the site and Princess Anne attended a memorial service in Reading, where many of the victims had joined the train. On the Saturday after the crash, all major sporting events held a minute's silence in memory of the victims.

In October 1999, Lord Cullen was appointed to chair the Ladbroke Grove Rail Inquiry, which was held the following year. As both the Paddington and Southall crashes had reopened public debate on Automatic Train Protection, a separate joint inquiry considering the issue in the light of both crashes was also held in 2000. The Cullen Inquiry was carried out in two blocks of sittings, either side of this joint inquiry. The first block dealt with the accident itself, the second block dealt with the management and regulation of UK railway safety.

WHY WAS SIGNAL SN109 PASSED AT DANGER?

The immediate cause of the disaster was identified as the Turbo train passing signal SN109, which was located on overhead gantry 8, with four other signals serving other tracks. It was established that the signal had been showing a red aspect, and the preceding signal, SN87, had been showing a single yellow, which should have led the driver to be prepared for a red at SN109. However, because Turbo driver, Michael Hodder, had died in the accident, it was not possible to establish why he had passed the signal at danger. Hodder, 31, was inexperienced, having qualified as a driver only two weeks before the crash... and his driver training was found to be defective. It was later revealed that SN109 had been passed at danger on eight previous times in the last six years and that it was one of 22 in the country with an extremely poor SPAD record.

On the day of the crash, just after 8am, the bright sunshine would have been low and behind Hodder, with low sunlight reflecting off yellow aspects. Poor signal placement meant that Hodder would have seen sunlit yellow aspects of SN109 at a point where his view of the red aspect of SN109, although not of any other signal on gantry 8, was still obstructed. Indeed, since 1998 a campaign to have the signal SN109 properly sited had been running and Bristol HST drivers were rerouted so as not to pass this signal. The resulting inquiry into the Ladbroke Grove disaster considered it more probable than not that the poor siting of SN109, both in itself and in comparison with the other signals on and at gantry 8, allied to the effect of bright sunlight at a low angle, were factors that had led Hodder to believe that he had a proceed aspect.

DRIVER TRAINING WAS INADEQUATE

Thames Trains had inherited a driver-training package from British Rail, but in February 1999, a concerned incoming training manager commissioned an external audit. It reported: "The trainers did not appear to be following the training course syllabus and supporting notes as they considered these to be 'not fit for purpose' with inappropriate time allowances for some sessions. The traction and introduction to the driving section of the course has been extended and the six-week route learning session is being used as additional practical handling." Driver Michael Hodder's 16 weeks of practical training had been given by a trainer who felt that, "I was not there to teach... the routes. I was totally to teach... how to drive a Turbo; the training manager was unaware of this."

Details of signals, which had been repeatedly passed at danger, should have been supplied to trainers and passed on to trainees, yet no trainer had done so. This practical trainer was unaware that SN109 was a multi-SPAD signal. Under the previous British Railways' training regime, trainees would have spent far longer in training and, once qualified, were not allowed to drive over the notoriously difficult approach to Paddington until they had at least two years' experience on less-complex routes. Hodder – a former Royal Navy gunner and first Gulf War veteran who left the service in 1996 on health grounds after dislocating a shoulder – had only qualified 13 days earlier. He had no previous experience as a railway worker, but no special attention was paid to this in either training or testing.

TRAIN PROTECTION "NOT BEEN IMPLEMENTED"

The Turbo had been fitted with Automatic Warning System apparatus requiring the driver to acknowledge a warning every time he approached a signal not at green. Yet if an Automatic Train Protection system had been fitted and working it would have automatically applied brakes to prevent the train going beyond any signal at red. National adoption of ATP, as preferred by British Rail, had been recommended after the Clapham Junction disaster, but subsequently abandoned because the safety benefits were considered not great enough to justify the cost. Following a previous SPAD, Thames Trains had commissioned a cost-benefit analysis study of the Paddington situation, which reached the same conclusion. The Ladbroke Grove accident showed beyond doubt that in both cases, this stance was wrong.

Written instructions for Railtrack signalling centre staff at Slough stipulated that as soon as they realised that a train had passed a signal at danger, they should set signals to danger and immediately send a radio 'emergency all stop' signal to the driver of the train by Cab Secure Radio. Yet in this case, it was only when the Class 165 was 200 yards past the signal did the signalmen begin to send such a radio signal. Their understanding of the instructions was that they should wait to see if the driver stopped of his own accord before attempting to contact him, and this interpretation was supported by their immediate manager. The signalmen had never been trained in the use of CSR, nor had they ever used it in response to a SPAD.

Statutory body the HM Railway Inspectorate itself was criticised for its inspection procedures. Its parent body, the Health and Safety Executive, was concerned about not only the length of time taken for the approval of the signalling scheme and the slow progress by Railtrack and the HMRI in bringing issues to a conclusion, but also the inadequate risk analysis. Part of the blame was laid on a lack of resources at HMRI, and its lack of vigour in pursuing issues. Only two weeks before the Ladbroke Grove disaster, the Health and Safety Executive announced an intention to require the adoption of Train Protection and Warning Systems. TPWS is an upgrade of Automatic Warning System, which could stop trains travelling at less than 70mph within the overlap distance of a red signal, delivering, according to HSE, about 65% of the safety benefits of Automatic Train Protection at much lower cost. The Health and Safety Executive specified that TPWS must be introduced by 2004, revising this date to 2003 after Ladbroke Grove. After the disaster, the rail industry and the general public alike became highly supportive of this measure.

RECORD FINES FOR THAMES TRAINS

On April 5, 2004, a record fine of £2 million was imposed on Thames Trains by Judge Mr Justice Bell at the Old Bailey for the company's part in the crash, after it pleaded guilty to two health and safety offences. Thames Trains was also ordered to pay prosecution costs of £75,000. The judge said that Thames Trains accepted that there had been "serious failures and omissions" on its part, but added: "There is significant mitigation in respect of Thames Trains' attitude to drivers and driver information and safety generally and its attitude to the disaster once it had occurred. I accept that Thames Trains had, and continues to have, a positive safety culture going specifically beyond minimum industry standards in a number of respects and demonstrated by its actions in a number of respects before the disaster and its conduct since."
On March 30, 2007, Network Rail received the biggest fine in its history after Judge Mr Justice Bean, sitting at Blackfriars Crown Court, imposed a £4 million penalty for its part in the disaster. But the scale of the fine failed to satisfy the bereaved families of the 31 who were killed. Network Rail had also pleaded guilty on October 31, 2006, to charges under the Health and Safety at Work Act 1974, but argued that it had been less culpable than Thames Trains. However, the judge dismissed such claims, saying that as successor to Railtrack, Network Rail's were, "far graver" than those of the train operator. It was also ordered to pay £225,000 in costs.

Driver Hodder's widow, Kerry, who discovered that she was pregnant with their third child a week after the death of her husband, spoke out after the court case for the first time, condemning Network Rail for "vilifying" him. "He was a victim as much as anyone else," she said. "The bosses at Network Rail, or Railtrack as it was then, had known for years that the signal outside Paddington station was dangerous, yet they did nothing about it. He was led into a rat-trap and there was no way out."

Away from the court case, HM Railway Inspectorate required the national adoption of TPWS apparatus, and incorporated the prohibition of British Railways Mk.1 rolling stock (which when introduced in the early 1950s had been hailed as a major safety innovation). Lord Cullen's recommendations in his inquiry led to the creation in 2003 of the Rail Safety and Standards Board and in 2005 of the Rail Accident Investigation Branch, separate from, but in addition to, HMRI. Signal SN109 was brought back into service in February 2006. It, along with many other signals in the Paddington area, is now a single-lens type signal. A memorial garden was set up, partially overlooking the crash site, and accessible from the adjacent Sainsbury's supermarket car park.

Chapter 29

2000 HATFIELD: CRACKED RAIL KILLER

T he fatal accident on the East Coast Main Line at Hatfield on October 17, 2000, in which four passengers died, was by no means one of the highest on the UK rail network in terms of loss of life. Yet its implications reached into every corner of the national network and brought about the demise of Railtrack, the post-privatisation infrastructure-owning company that had succeeded British Rail.

A Great North Eastern Railway InterCity 225 set bound for Leeds with 170 passengers on board left King's Cross at 12.10pm, and was travelling at 117mph when it became derailed south of Hatfield station 23 minutes later. The cause was a cracked rail. No. 91023, the leading Class 91 locomotive, and the first two coaches did not derail but stayed upright. However, all those behind them, including the Driving Van Trailer, came off the tracks as the set split into three sections. The eighth vehicle in the set was the restaurant car. It overturned on to its side and hit an overhead power line gantry, causing extensive damage. The four passengers who died in the crash were all in the restaurant car, and 70 more sustained injuries.

A week later, a minute's silence was held to mark the Hatfield rail crash, with stations and trains along the route of the doomed train taking part. In 2003, six individuals and Network Rail (as the successor to Railtrack) and the division of engineering giant Balfour Beatty, which maintained the track, were charged with manslaughter in connection with the Hatfield derailment. Some of the charges against Network Rail/Railtrack and certain of its executives were dropped in September 2004, but the other charges stood. The trial began in January 2005 and was set to last a year. A backlog of essential work had been allowed to accumulate and the cracked rail had been identified for repair 21 months earlier, the jury heard. Prosecutors said the accident had been the result of a "cavalier approach" to safety. However, on July 14, the judge, Mr Justice Mackay, instructed the jury to acquit all defendants on charges of manslaughter. Several days later, after the corporate manslaughter charge was thrown out, Balfour Beatty changed its plea to guilty on the health and safety charges. On September 6, Network Rail was found guilty of breaching health and safety law. All of the executives were acquitted.

On October 7, 2005, the court imposed record penalties on the two companies. Balfour Beatty was fined £10 million and Network Rail £3.5 million for breaking safety rules before the crash. Each company was ordered to pay £300,000 each in legal costs. Mr Justice Mackay said that Balfour Beatty's breaches of the Health and Safety Act were, "one of the worst examples of sustained industrial negligence..." "Hatfield was a tragedy, and our thoughts remain with the bereaved families and with those injured and otherwise affected by it," the company said in a statement. "Balfour Beatty Rail Infrastructure Services, in entering its plea of guilty, accepted inadequacies in its patrolling and inspection services, for which it apologises. It is, however, clear that the accident arose as a result of a systematic failure of the industry as a whole. At no stage did BBRIS work outside the industry standards on patrolling and inspection as they were constituted before the accident."

A NATIONAL PROBLEM

Preliminary investigation discovered that a rail had fragmented as trains passed and that the likely cause was "rolling contact fatigue," defined as multiple surface-breaking cracks. Such cracks are caused by high loads where the wheels contact the rail. Repeated loading causes fatigue cracks to grow, and when they reach a critical size, the rail fails. More than 300 critical cracks were found in rails at Hatfield. The problem was known about before the accident, and replacement rails had been made available, but had not been delivered to the correct location for installation. Fears that other rails might be similarly affected, meant that speed restrictions were imposed on huge lengths of track on the entire network, causing significant delays on many routes, while checks were carried out.

The number of cracks similar to those found at Hatfield throughout the UK was astonishingly high. At the time, the rail infrastructure company responsible for the national network was Railtrack, the post-privatisation successor to British Rail. Railtrack had in turn hired contractors to do the maintenance work, which had once been part and parcel of British Rail's responsibilities. That strategy left Railtrack bereft of adequate maintenance records and no accessible asset register. It did not know how many other cases of rolling contact fatigue around the network could lead to a Hatfield-like accident. So, it imposed more than 1,200 emergency speed restrictions and instigated a nationwide track replacement programme, which led to delays for more than a year on many parts of the network. In this respect, the company was subject to 'enforcement' by the Rail Regulator, Tom Winsor. Ironically, just before the crash, new figures from Railtrack's safety and standards directorate had shown that nationally, the number of derailments had been falling. The post-Hatfield delays caused profits by train operating companies across the network to fall by 19% in the 12 months after the crash. Freight operator English, Welsh & Scottish Railway cancelled up to 400 trains per week as a result, while Freightliner's losses resulting from the delays were estimated at £1 million per month. In all, the cost to the national economy of the delays was estimated at £6 million per day.

THE DEMISE OF RAILTRACK

Railtrack was the name given to the group of companies which owned the track, signalling, tunnels, bridges, level crossings and virtually all of the stations on the national network from 1994. It was listed on the London Stock Exchange, and was a constituent of the FTSE 100 Index. But Hatfield delivered the company a death blow, leaving it with a huge bill to inspect the entire system for defects. In 2001, Railtrack announced that, despite making a pre-tax profit before exceptional expenses of £199 million, the £733 million of costs and compensation paid out over the Hatfield crash plunged Railtrack from profit to a loss of £534 million. It had to resort to approaching the government with a begging bowl, and then angered many by using the funding it received to pay a £137 million dividend to its shareholders in May 2001.

Railtrack's spiralling costs led to the collapse of the company, which entered administration at the insistence of Transport Secretary Stephen Byers MP, two years after Hatfield. It was replaced under Byers's successor Alistair Darling MP by a not-for-dividend company that was in part state owned – Network Rail – formed with the principal purpose of acquiring and owning Railtrack plc, which it did on October 3, 2002. Railtrack plc was subsequently renamed Network Rail Infrastructure Limited. At the time, groups that represented British train passengers welcomed the move. Also in 2002, the Institute of Rail Welding was established by The Welding Institute and Network Rail in response to the recommendations in the report into the Hatfield crash, with the aim of facilitating best practice.

————————— *Chapter 30* —————————

2001 GREAT HECK: TEN PEOPLE DIED – AND THE RAILWAY WAS BLAMELESS

The worst UK rail accident of the 21st century was at Great Heck in Yorkshire, where 10 people lost their lives, in a tragedy said to have had a 67-billion-to-one chance of happening and that the railway could have done little, if anything, to have foreseen or prevented it.

The chances of winning the jackpot in the UK National Lottery have been quoted at one in 14 million. NASA estimates the odds of a person being hit by a piece of space debris are around one in 3,200. Those odds are higher still of getting a hole in one if you play golf, which are estimated at 5,000 to one. The chances of being struck by lightning in a lifetime are 10,000 to one while the odds of being killed by a shark are said to be 300,000,000 to one. So, what are the chances of setting out on a motorway journey, veering off the road at the wrong place at the wrong time, crashing through barriers, rolling down an embankment, ending up on one of the country's busiest railway lines and causing a high-speed crash involving two trains and claiming the lives of 10 people and seriously injuring 82 more? Experts placed the chances of that happening at 67 billion to one. Yet it still happened, at 6.13am on February 28, 2001.

The Great Heck or Selby rail crash on the East Coast Main Line remains the worst UK rail disaster of the 21st century. The pivotal figure in the crash was 36-year-old Lincolnshire builder Gary Neil Hart. He was driving a Land Rover Defender which, while towing a loaded trailer carrying a Renault Savanna estate car, swerved off the westbound M62 just before an overbridge on the line at Great Heck. The Land Rover ran down an embankment and on to the southbound track. Hart tried to reverse it off the track, but he could not, using his mobile telephone to call the emergency services from the lineside after leaving the vehicle. Two minutes later, the Land Rover was hit by a Great North Eastern Railway InterCity 225 set comprising the 4.45am Newcastle to King's Cross service, propelled by Class 91 locomotive No. 91023 and led by Driving Van Trailer No. 82221, and carrying 99 passengers and crew. If not for the early start, it is likely that there would have been many more on the train.

After striking the Land Rover a glancing blow, which threw it on to the side of the track, the leading bogie of the DVT derailed, but the train stayed upright. It careered through an occupation bridge and continued for about a quarter of a mile as its driver desperately made an emergency brake application. However, points to nearby sidings then deflected the 225 into the path of an oncoming Freightliner coal train running from Immingham to Ferrybridge behind Class 66 No. 66521. The freight train hit the passenger train approximately half a mile from the impact with the Land Rover. Investigators later said that only one axle may have come off the rails. Had that section of line been plain track, without those points, the 225 might have been able to carry on until the driver could slow it to a halt.

The impact resulted in the near destruction of the lightweight DVT and extensive damage to all nine of the 225's coaches, which mostly overturned and came to rest down an embankment to the east side of the track, in a field near the line. The trailing locomotive remained upright and suffered minor damage, although it was derailed, but the impact was so severe that the Class 66 lost its bogies, with debris of the DVT jammed underneath rupturing its fuel tank. The 66 then overturned on to its left side and slid across the front gardens of Station Terrace, crushing a caravan, a garden shed, workshop and summerhouse, coming to a halt just yards short of family homes, in a garden. The first nine wagons following it were also derailed and damaged to varying extents. Before the two trains collided, the speed of the InterCity 225 was estimated at 88mph and that of the freight train as 54mph. With an estimated closing speed of 142 mph (229kmh), the collision between the trains is the highest speed railway incident that has occurred in the UK.

Both train drivers, John Weddle (GNER) and Stephen (George) Dunn (Freightliner), two InterCity 225 crew members, guard Raymond Robson and chef Paul Taylor, as well as six passengers, died, all as a result of the second collision. However, train-driving instructor Andrew Hill, who was travelling in the cab of No. 66521 and teaching a new route to the driver of the Class 66, survived. Emergency services were on the scene within 40 minutes, but by then many local residents had rushed out of their homes to locate and help the survivors. When the emergency services arrived at the scene, in addition to helping the injured, they carried out disinfecting procedures as there was an outbreak of foot and mouth disease at the time. Doctors and nurses who were about to end their night shifts in local hospitals responded by setting up a 'triage' in a field to give on-the-spot treatment to the injured, a procedure used only in battlefield conditions. The wounded were taken to a nearby barn and comforted by two local clergy. By 9am, fire crews had detected an unexpected hint of life in an unreachable section of train between two crushed coaches. Thermal imaging equipment confirmed that a passenger was stuck and officers drilled a hole in the carriage roof and dropped a vibraphone digital video camera in a bid to find her, which they did, and at 1pm she was the last to be removed.

A total of 82 survivors were taken to hospital. The official incident report praised the crashworthiness of the InterCity 225's Mk.4 coaches, without which the death toll might have been higher. By coincidence, No. 91023 had also been involved in the Hatfield rail crash four months earlier, also escaping with only slight damage. It was later renumbered 91132. Another coincidence was that the crash occurred exactly 46 years to the day after the Moorgate disaster, as described in Chapter 22.

A FATAL CHAIN OF EVENTS SPARKED OFF

Gary Hart, however, was uninjured. He later said that while he had witnessed the impact between the InterCity 225 and his Land Rover, he had not been aware of the more serious collision with the coal train until told by police several hours later. At first, he claimed that the Land Rover had suffered a mechanical fault, or had collided with an object on the road. An investigation, including reconstruction of the car to demonstrate that it was not mechanically defective, concluded that Hart had been driving in a sleep-deprived condition, and had not applied the brakes as it went down the embankment. It later emerged that Hart, who at the time had split from his wife Elaine, had stayed up the previous night talking on the telephone to a 40-year-old Scunthorpe woman he had met through an internet dating agency.

At Leeds Crown Court, Hart was tried on 10 counts of causing death by dangerous driving. He admitted in court that he led an "unusual" lifestyle, often skipping breakfast and lunch and claiming that he could go without a break for 36 hours. He had told police in one interview: "My life is 1000 miles per hour. It's just the way I live." At the time, Hart, who was described as a "hard-working boss of his own construction firm," was living in a bungalow in Strubby, a village near Mablethorpe, while his wife lived nine miles away in Louth. Eight days before the crash, he had started an internet and telephone friendship with the Scunthorpe woman, and they had been due to meet on the night of the crash. The day before the crash, the pair had spent five hours talking to each other on the telephone, and Hart told police that the conversation had left him "buzzing with excitement" and unable to sleep. He then set off in the Land Rover at 4.40am but denied that he fell asleep at the wheel, saying instead that he lost control after hearing a noise in the vehicle.

Prosecutor James Goss QC told Leeds Crown Court that Hart's bad driving, caused by his lack of sleep, was responsible for the 10 deaths, stating that Hart had said that he didn't have any sleep the night before the accident, and that he did not even go to bed. Judge Mr Justice Mackay said the rail crash was, "perhaps the worst driving-related incident in the UK in recent years." Hart walked into the courtroom to hear the verdicts hand-in-hand with his wife Elaine, with whom he had become reconciled with. He was found guilty on all 10 counts. As the jury foreman read out the verdicts, Hart held his head in his hands. He was sentenced to five years in prison, and served 30 months before early release.

In April 2003, three appeal court judges threw out an attempt by Hart to challenge the five-year jail sentence. Hart had claimed that the jury's verdict was unsafe, because six witnesses had said he was driving in a "sensible and appropriate" manner before the accident. He also argued that the trial judge should not have ruled out an alternative verdict of driving carelessly. However, Lord Justice Rose, sitting with Mr Justice Mitchell and Mr Justice Eady, ruled that there was, "no reason whatever to regard these verdicts as unsafe." After release, Hart continued to deny having fallen asleep at the wheel, as the jury clearly decided that he had. He later said: "There's not a day gone by that I haven't thought about Selby. There's an awful lot of guilt attached with the accident. I do feel for the families because it was a horrendous, horrible way to go, die. I was nearly there myself."

He said that others should have shared in responsibility for the tragedy, as the deaths, "all occurred 700 yards down the track, which I feel other people should have been held accountable for, so in my own head I've dealt with it in that fashion." Campaigners claimed that the crash barriers alongside the M62 at that point were not long enough. Yet a Highways Agency review of crash barriers on bridges over railways published in 2003 concluded that only three bridges nationwide were in need of upgrading. The bridge at Great Heck was not one of them. Gary Hart's insurers, through Hart's name, sued the Department for Transport for a contribution to the damages they were liable to pay to GNER and the victims, on the grounds that the safety barrier was inadequate, and on legal grounds of contributory negligence, but the case was dismissed. The insurers paid out more than £22 million.

HOW ON EARTH CAN IT BE PREVENTED FROM HAPPENING AGAIN?
Deputy Prime Minister John Prescott asked the Highways Agency to review its standards for nearside safety barriers. He also asked the Health and Safety Commission to convene a working group to look at the circumstances of incidents where vehicles had blocked rail lines and whether there are features in common that might have been preventable. Its subsequent report 'Obstruction of the railway by road vehicles' was published on February 25, 2002. It concluded that, "the risk is small in relation to other elements of railway risk and tiny in relation to other elements of road risk," saying that, "schemes to reduce risks of road vehicles ending up on railway lines should not leapfrog other

road and rail safety initiatives that would yield bigger safety improvements; and at many locations there may be nothing more to be done beyond what is already in place." However, the report said that road authorities should seriously consider building safety fences appropriate to the type of site, the level and type of traffic. "Risk here should be reduced to a level that is as low as reasonably practicable. The key is deciding the right level of investment to meet this principle. The measures that are most likely to be implemented to prevent road and rail fatalities and injuries are either safety fencing, or changes in road marking, signing or traffic management."

The report quoted figures, which showed that on average, 0.1 train occupants and 0.4 vehicle occupants die in Great Britain every year as a result of accidental incursions on to Network Rail's railway lines, excluding accidents at level crossings. Gary Hart may never have dreamed of hurting anyone, yet the tragedy reinforced the point that driving while tired or having had no sleep can be as fatal as driving under the influence of drink or drugs. That is why there are tachographs in lorries.

If, as the prosecution claimed, and the jury chose to believe, Hart did fall asleep at the wheel, in theory he could just as easily have caused a multiple pile-up on the motorway. So, how can railways realistically guarantee the prevention of a similar "67-billion-to-one" event, the root cause of which they were blameless? In response to the tragedy, road safety charity Brake carried out a survey which found that 45% of drivers had got behind the wheel in the previous year after having less than five hours' sleep. It might be said we've all done it at some time or other, but we shouldn't. Ever. So, how do we get that message across?

REMEMBERING THE VICTIMS
The 10th anniversary was marked by a church service at St Paul's Church in Hensall, near Selby, attended by relatives, survivors and rail staff, followed by a private memorial service for relatives and rail staff in the memorial garden which has been laid close to the trackside at Great Heck. Locomotive No. 66526 has since been named *Driver Steve Dunn (George)* and carries a plaque that reads: "In remembrance of a dedicated engineman Driver Steve (George) Dunn tragically killed in the accident at Great Heck on 28th February 2001." His son James, who was nine at the time of the crash, later became a train driver himself. Driver John Weddle had a new driver training school in his home city of Newcastle named after him. His 16-year-old daughter Stephanie unveiled a plaque dedicating the school to his memory. Passenger Barry Needham, a freight logistics coordinator from York, was also commemorated as No. 60087 was named after him; the plates later being transferred to No. 60091, which carries an explanatory plaque.

————————— *Chapter 31* —————————

2002 POTTERS BAR: THEY WAITED NINE YEARS FOR JUSTICE

Had a set of points been properly checked at Potters Bar station, a crash that left seven people dead on May 10, 2002, would not have happened. The disaster led to rail maintenance being taken back from the private sector into the hands of state-owned Network Rail.

The station, on the East Coast Main Line, has been the scene of three major accidents. The first occurred on March 19, 1898, when the 7.50pm from Hatfield to King's Cross passed signals at danger, overrode the catch points, cut through the buffers and crashed on to the platform. The front part of the engine was smashed and the leading coach wrecked. The driver, fireman and guard narrowly escaped injury, and while passengers complained of being shaken up, nobody died. February 10, 1946, saw a local passenger train bound for King's Cross hit a set of buffers at the station, derailing the carriages and blocking the main line. Two express trains travelling in opposite directions then hit the wreckage. Two passengers died and 17 were injured and taken to hospital. While the driver of the local train was eventually blamed, a signalman contributed to the accident by changing a set of points as the train passed over them.

The third accident occurred on May 10, 2002, after the 12.45pm West Anglia Great Northern London King's Cross to King's Lynn service, comprising Class 365 Electric Multiple Unit No. 365526, with 151 passengers on board, left King's Cross, and 11 minutes later, at a speed of 97mph, crossed over 2182A, the set of points just south of Potters Bar station. As the end coach went over the points, they moved, and the rear bogie crossed over on to the line alongside. The bogie derailed at speed, flipping it into the air, and carried the vehicle into the station. The carriage hit a bridge parapet, scattering masonry on to Darkes Lane beneath, killing one pedestrian, 80-year-old Agnes Quinlivan. The coach then mounted the platform and slid along it before finally stopping at 45 degrees beneath the canopy. The front three coaches stayed upright, and came to a stop north of the station. Six passengers in the stricken carriage died.

Driver Gordon Gibson, known as Andy, and signal inspector Roger Badger, who had both been in the cab of the fated EMU, used circuit clips to warn the signal office at King's Cross and track detonators to alert other drivers. The driver also helped a seriously injured passenger out of the train with ladders. Michael Baker, platform supervisor at Potters Bar, warned incoming trains and ensured the live overhead cables were turned off. Alan Williams, the driver of a train travelling towards Potters Bar from the north, managed to stop before hitting the derailed carriage. He alighted and helped other trapped passengers escape. Gordon Gibson, who had been driving the EMU, said in a statement he realised there had been a derailment after feeling a "dragging sensation" followed by three jolts. He added: "I pressed the emergency button but it was dead."

RAF Wing Commander Martin Rose, a passenger inside the first-class section of the derailed rear coach, said that it flipped over and over "like a tumble dryer" before coming to a halt. He blacked out momentarily after being "tossed around", but quickly recovered, got up and checked for fire before going to help an elderly couple, author Nina Bawden and her husband Austen Kark, who were trapped. The pilot made attempts to pull Mr Kark out from where he had become trapped, but when he realised the 75-year-old was not going to regain consciousness, he diverted his attention to saving Nina's life, keeping her talking and awake.

Waiting passengers from the station platforms came to the aid of the injured. Off-duty police officer David Bedford leapt on to the tracks and smashed two of the carriage's windows with lumps of broken concrete. Sally Hatton, hairdresser at Potters Bar's Sunshine Hairdressers, had grabbed her first-aid kit as soon as she heard that there had been a crash, and on her way to the station, she tended victim Agnes Quinlivan, who had been fatally injured by falling debris. Staff at nearby Sainsbury's turned their store into a makeshift hospital. Hertfordshire Police later made arrangements to allow relatives of those who had died in the crash to lay flowers on the track.

SABOTAGE CLAIMS DID NOT STAND UP

In a report released in May the following year, the Health and Safety Executive said that the points had been poorly maintained and that this was the principal cause of the accident. Four bolts holding the stretcher bars that keep the rails apart had come loose or gone missing, resulting in the points moving while the train passed over them. The points had been fully inspected nine days before by a team working for the private maintenance firm Jarvis Rail and there had been a further visual inspection the day before the crash, with no problems reported. Railtrack was alerted to a problem on the line at Potters Bar just hours before the crash, after a rail worker travelling on the Down line had reported "lethal vibrations" on the track while going over point 2182A. A safety manager sent staff to investigate, but owing to an inadequate incident reporting system, they instead went to the Up line, and so did not find the reported "loose nuts" that caused the fatal accident the same day.

At first, Jarvis claimed that the points had been sabotaged, producing photographs and analysis which, it claimed, amounted to evidence that the set of damaged points had been tampered with. The claim was dismissed by police and caused outrage among survivors, who said they believed inadequate maintenance was the reason four safety-critical bolts were missing from the points. Indeed, no concrete evidence to support this theory ever emerged. Indeed, the HSE investigation discovered that other sets of points in the Potters Bar area showed similar if lesser maintenance deficiencies. The report said that the poor state of maintenance "probably arose from a failure to understand fully the design and safety requirements". The HSE found that heavy and constant vibrations on the stretcher bars and their bolts caused them in turn to vibrate and oscillate — until their nuts literally fell off the bolts. These have since been replaced by two-part locking nuts instead of the main nuts with half-size locking nuts to hold them in place. In the wake of the disaster, it was widely debated about whether private maintenance firms were paying too little attention to training and safety.

A PRIVATISATION U-TURN

Accordingly, in 2003, Network Rail announced it was taking all track maintenance in-house, ending the use of private contractors except for large-scale renewal or development projects. On April 28, 2004, Jarvis sent a letter to the victims' families, admitting liability for the accident. The company said that it would formally accept "legally justified claims" after making a financial provision of £3 million. It also apologised for claiming that sabotage had caused the accident. Chief executive Kevin Hyde wrote: "In the aftermath of the crash, when Jarvis was under great pressure to explain itself, we were drawn into a debate about the possible causes of the crash. On behalf of the company and my colleagues, I would like to apologise for the hurt and anger our actions in responding caused." Novelist Nina Bawden, who suffered serious injuries and lost her husband Austen Kark in the crash, asked: "Why did Jarvis insist for so long that little green men were responsible for the crash?" She said that the two companies' admission of liability was "welcome news" because survivors had previously been refused legal aid and would have had to find their own money to sue for compensation. The Office of Rail Regulation stated: "Jarvis's performance fell far short of that to be expected."

At its peak, Jarvis Rail was responsible for maintaining a quarter of Britain's rail network. On September 16, 2003, a GNER express was derailed at just after 7am, immediately after leaving Platform 4 at King's Cross station, because a missing length of rail had been removed during maintenance work. It should not have been possible for a train to be routed on to the section of track where the rail had been removed. The significance of this accident was not in the accident itself, which was not serious, but in the political consequences for the private contractor, Jarvis plc, employed to maintain the track. The company's reputation was further blackened, and Jarvis quit rail maintenance, marking the end of private company-led rail maintenance in the UK, with all future work being administered by state-owned Network Rail. In March 2010, Jarvis announced that it was to enter administration, after lenders refused to offer the company further credit to continue trading as a going concern. As a consequence of the Hatfield and Potters Bar disasters, Network Rail was forced to bring back in-house maintenance activities. The National Union of Rail, Maritime and Transport Workers' general secretary, the late Bob Crow, said: "People need to remember that it was the privatised Railtrack and their contractors who were responsible for the Potters Bar disaster and that Network Rail have been left to sweep up the mess."

THE FINE WE ALL PAID
On June 1, 2010, Judge Michael Findlay Baker QC opened the inquest into the disaster; it was held at the Spirella Building in Letchworth, Hertfordshire. On July 30, the jury found that the crash had occurred because of a points failure caused by their unsafe condition, adding that there were failures of inspection and/or maintenance of the points in the period before the crash. The coroner said he would file a report warning of continued risk of other deaths on the rail network, and criticised the "indefensible" length of time families of the victims had had to wait for an inquest to be held. "Whatever the causes, the passage of over eight years from the derailment to the conclusion of the hearing of the inquest is indefensible," he said. Bob Crow, general secretary of the Rail, Maritime and Transport Union, said it was "an absolute scandal" that it had taken eight years to hold an inquest. "This tragic loss of life at Potters Bar could have been avoided if safety rather than profits had been the priority on our railways back in May 2002. Basic failures of inspection and of maintenance, driven by the greed and fragmentation of rail privatisation, led us to Potters Bar."

On November 9, it was announced that Network Rail and Jarvis, the maintenance contractor, were to be prosecuted on health and safety grounds over the condition of the tracks. Network Rail inherited liability for the crash from its privately owned predecessor, Railtrack. At Watford magistrates court on February 21, 2011, Network Rail said it would plead guilty to health and safety failings. However, following that plea, the Office of Rail Regulation decided not to proceed with the prosecution of Jarvis Rail because it was not in the public interest, as there was no value in convicting a company that had gone into administration as insolvent, and would therefore not be in a position to pay fines. Louise Christian, a solicitor who had represented the families of the victims at the inquest, said: "These criminal proceedings are a bit of a charade. They deliver no accountability. The only person paying the fine is the taxpayer." At the time Network Rail's main funding was an annual government grant of nearly £4 billion. That may well have been, but on May 13, 2011, at St Albans Crown Court, Network Rail was fined £3 million by Judge Andrew Bright QC for the safety failings.

Pat Smith, whose 80-year-old mother Agnes Quinlivan was killed by falling debris as she walked under the bridge, said: "I just hope that other families in the future are not treated as shabbily as we were by the rail companies, and I include Network Rail in that. There has been total disregard for the bereaved families." The judge said he was required by law to impose a fine that reflected the "financial circumstances of the offender" but said he would reduce the amount because he knew Network Rail was financed from public funds. "In reality, therefore, every pound of any fine will be one pound that cannot be spent on railway safety," he said. A Network Rail spokesman said after the hearing: "We say again today that we are truly sorry. Private contractors are no longer in control of the day-to-day maintenance of the nation's rail infrastructure since Network Rail took this entire operation in-house in 2004. Today the railways are safer than they have ever been, yet our task remains to build on that record and always to learn any lessons we can to make it ever safer for passengers and those who work on the railway." Ian Prosser, director of rail safety at the Office of Rail Regulation, said after the court case: "Safety on Britain's railways has improved significantly over the last nine years and today statistics show we have one of the safest railways in Europe."

A memorial service took place on May 10, 2012, to mark the 10th anniversary of the Potters Bar rail crash. Survivors and the families of the victims gathered in the memorial garden, which has been laid outside the station, and were joined by members of the emergency services and those who simply wanted to pay their respects. A minute's silence was held at 12.56pm, the time the train derailed.

——————————— *Chapter 32* ———————————

2004 UFTON NERVET: THEY WAITED 12 YEARS FOR A BRIDGE

The half-barrier level crossing at Ufton Nervet in west Berkshire had become notorious for suicide attempts, one of which caused the deaths of a High Speed Train driver and six passengers on November 6, 2004. Yet it took 12 years for a replacement bridge to be provided.

We may never know exactly why hotel chef Brian Drysdale decided to kill himself by parking his Mazda 323 on the automatic level crossing on the Great Western Main Line on that day. His actions caused First Great Western's 5.35pm service from Paddington to Plymouth, comprising an InterCity 125 High Speed Train led by Class 43 power car No. 43019, and with 281 people on board, to crash into his car. The rear of the train came to rest about 110 yards beyond the crossing with all eight coaches derailed. The driver of the train, Stanley Martin, and five passengers died, and another 71 of those on board were injured, 12 of them seriously. Survivors reported using safety hammers to break the train windows after the collision. The incident occurred after dark and passengers used mobile phones to provide light. More than 20 ambulances from five counties and 14 fire engines attended the crash and 11 people were cut free from the wreckage. A total of 61 injured people were taken to the Royal Berkshire Hospital in Reading and others to the North Hampshire Hospital in Basingstoke. Those who sustained minor injuries were treated at the scene and the Winning Hand pub. The high structural integrity of the Mk.3 coaches prevented a much higher death toll, plus the fact that the more lightly loaded first-class coaches were at the leading end of the train.

The crash, investigation and repairs blocked the main railway route between London and the West Country until the morning of November 16, after which temporary speed restrictions were imposed to allow the bedding in of ballast. In the meantime, inter-city trains operated via Swindon and Westbury and local services were replaced by rail and bus shuttles. The automated crossing was of a half-barrier type, with red and white stripes used on roads where traffic is unlikely to queue across the crossing and where rail line-speed is not more than 100mph. There are no means of checking that the crossing is not obstructed before the passage of a train. The half barriers close the left-hand carriageway to traffic approaching the crossing, but allow any vehicle still crossing to escape. However, this does not physically prevent road users from zigzagging around the barriers and crossing the line, usually in an attempt to save time.

A preliminary report by the Health and Safety Executive indicated that Drysdale, 48, who worked at the nearby Wokefield Park Hotel near Reading, stopped on the crossing before any warnings and failed to react to the barrier alarm sequence. A minor deflection of his stationary car to one side by the train derailed the forward bogie, with horrendous consequences. A report from the Rail Safety and Standards Board recommended improved emergency communications at the level crossing and the relocation of a set of points, the position of which had been a factor in the train's derailment. Network Rail implemented all the safety recommendations. A support group, the Ufton Nervet Train Crash Network, was set up for survivors and relatives of the victims. In 2005 the Royal

Humane Society awarded its bronze medal to two passengers, salesman Brian Kemsley and Royal Marines Company Sergeant Major Tom McPhee, for helping the wounded and dying on board, including a nine-year-old girl and her mother who both died after having been thrown out of the train by the force of the crash.

On November 1, 2007, a month-long inquest at the Guildhall in Windsor returned verdicts that the crash was caused by Drysdale's successful attempt at suicide, and that the driver and six passengers had been unlawfully killed. The inquest heard that Drysdale had been to work at the hotel on the day of the crash, but left early at 5.30pm, saying he was ill. He left a note telling the Sunday chef what food to order. Less than 45 minutes later, he was seen to move his car between the gates at the level crossing a few miles away. It was revealed at the hearing that Drysdale was awaiting the results of an HIV test when the crash happened. The results later revealed that he was negative. The inquest heard that Drysdale was homosexual, but had hidden his sexuality from friends and family for years. A former boyfriend said: "He said he couldn't come to terms with his sexuality and was, in his view, tormented by it."

The British Transport Police officer leading the investigation into the crash said that if Drysdale had survived, he would have pushed for his prosecution on manslaughter or potentially murder charges. However, 2004 had not seen the first deaths at the crossing, nor would they be the last. In 2009 a man from Reading took his own life at the crossing by jumping in front of a train. The following year, a man from Fareham was killed by a train on the crossing; the British Transport Police concluded that his death was not suspicious. On May 22, 2012, an express hit a motor scooter on the crossing, killing the rider, David Montague. The British Transport Police reported that the crossing was working correctly, but an inquest resulted in an open verdict because of insufficient evidence that the rider had intended suicide. On October 16, 2014, a man from Calcot, Berkshire, was struck and killed by a train, police again concluding that the circumstances were not suspicious.

THE CROSSING REPLACED

Survivors of the 2004 crash, local councillors, safety campaigners and the National Union of Rail, Maritime and Transport Workers repeatedly demanded either full barriers or a replacement bridge at the crossing. In July 2012, an internet petition was started by Liberal Democrat members of West Berkshire Council and a Hungerford resident to lobby for full barriers and closed circuit television to be installed. Network Rail looked at providing a bridge, but in November 2012, said it needed more funding. In March 2014, John Redwood, Conservative MP for Wokingham, said that an apology to families bereaved by level crossing accidents was "better late than never". The apology came as a report strongly criticised Network Rail's handling of tragedies in the past. Ian Prosser, director of railway safety at the Office of Rail & Road, said that changes to the Ufton Nervet crossing were overdue. In August 2015, the council passed plans for a road bridge to replace the crossing. Building work finally began in 2016 and the £7 million bridge opened on December 16 that year.

The scheme involved moving the garden set up in memory of the 2004 crash from the south to the north side of the crossing to make it more accessible. The memorial garden is now next to that dedicated to driver Stanley Martin. Survivor Jane Hawker said that the closure of the old crossing meant the area can become "a peaceful country place again". She was one of two passengers to open the new bridge in a ceremony. She added: "As a survivor of the 2004 crash, I will always live with the memories and the consequences, but the closure of the crossing means that I will no longer dread hearing about another incident happening there. It gives me a form of closure, and makes the area safer for the wider public. The recognition by Network Rail of the importance of building this bridge, at all levels of the organisation, has been liberating for me, and the personal dedication of all involved with the construction has been heart-warming." A Network Rail spokesman said that the level crossing had been "perfectly safe" if used correctly and that the tragedies had been a result of "misuse".

Chapter 33

2004 TEBAY: 'GREED' SET OFF A RUNAWAY TRAIN

Four railway workers were crushed by a runaway wagon at Tebay, in Cumbria, on the West Coast Main Line early on February 15, 2004, because a private contractor had disguised the fact the brakes were not working in a bid to save money.

The wagon, laden with lengths of rail, and parked at a maintenance area at Scout Green, had had its hydraulic brake disconnected after a fault, and it had not been repaired or replaced by rail maintenance company MAC Machinery Services. Instead, wooden chocks had been placed in front of the wagon to stop it moving. As crane operator Roy Kennett began using an excavator's log grab in an attempt to drag sections of scrap rail from the wagon, the wooden blocks dislodged. Slowly the 16-ton steel wagon began to move downhill gathering momentum on the 1-in-75 gradient from Shap summit in darkness. Running silently and without warning, the wagon reached speeds of up to 40mph.

Workers Colin Buckley, 49, Darren Burgess, 30, both from Carnforth, Chris Waters, 53, from Morecambe and Gary Tindall, 46, from Tebay, were carrying out overnight work 3¼ miles further down the main line from the depot, and because of noise from an on-site generator, had no warning of the wagon's approach. The four died after suffering massive injuries, including loss of limbs, and five other men were also injured. The wagon ran on for another four miles until it finally came to a halt.

MAC Machinery Services boss Mark Connolly from Anglesey, North Wales, and Roy Kennett from Maidstone, Kent, denied four counts of manslaughter when they appeared before Newcastle Crown Court in 2006. Connolly also denied three counts of breaching health and safety laws, and Kennett denied one count. Prosecuting, Robert Smith QC said that Connolly had deliberately disconnected the hydraulic brakes on two wagons because it was cheaper than repairing the wagons properly. The hydraulic systems were in such a bad way they would not work properly in conjunction with a crane. Mr Smith said: "Instead of repairing the trucks and the crane, he devised the simple but grossly irresponsible and dangerously expedient practice of dismantling these brakes." Connolly had driven a low-loader truck with a railway crane and two wagons to Scout Green in Cumbria to lift ageing track from the West Coast Main Line on to railway wagons. Connolly filled cables connecting the wagons to the crane – usually filled with hydraulic brake fluid – with ball bearings, giving the impression everything was above board. The court heard that Kennett was not qualified to operate the crane. He had placed the chocks beneath the wheels because he wanted to ensure they did not move as he unloaded the steel rails.

On March 17, 2006, both men were found guilty by majority verdicts. Connolly was sentenced to nine years' imprisonment and Kennett for two. Richard Lissack QC, defending Connolly, said that the father-of-two was a "broken man", having lost his home, business and family. However, outside the court, Superintendent Alistair Cumming of the British Transport Police condemned Connolly for his greed and "blatant and premeditated disregard for safety". The Rail, Maritime and Transport Union said that the case had shown how easily railway safety could be breached following Privatisation. After the pair were jailed, Detective Sergeant Steve Martin read a statement on behalf of all the families: "During the past two years we have had to come to terms with not only our loss, but also that this was an accident that could and should never have happened. We have been unable to understand how or why anyone would put onto the railway trailers which had had their brakes deliberately disabled. Even though the jury has delivered a guilty verdict, we have no sense of victory or celebration and our lives have changed forever."

On March 7, 2007, both men failed in a bid to get their convictions quashed at the Court of Appeal, arguing that the summing up in their trial was flawed. However, Connolly succeeded in winning a two-year reduction in his nine-year jail sentence. In February 2014, a decade after the tragedy, survivors and relatives of those killed said it was unacceptable that equipment designed to prevent a repeat had not been introduced, and that there had been several incidents of runaway trucks since Tebay. Ian Prosser, director of railway safety at the Office of Rail Regulation, said there had been "some" runaway incidents in previous years but fewer than previously. "There has been a significant amount of enforcement from my inspectors in the area of train protection and road-rail vehicles and that has pushed Network Rail to make the improvements that we see – but there's still more to do."

However, in February 2016, Mick Cash, general secretary of the National Union of Rail, Maritime and Transport Workers, again blamed privatisation for the tragedy and pledged to fight for rail workers' safety. "The events of that night came about as a direct result of the privatisation and fragmentation of our railways," he said. "Those dangers still exist on the railway today and RMT continues the fight for proper protection systems to be introduced right across the network. Twelve years after Tebay, we still have a mess of contractors, subcontractors and a host of labour-only agencies – often using zero-hour contracts in a race to the bottom." In 2014, a Network Rail spokesman said: "All the recommendations made by the independent safety investigator into the accident have been implemented. This means that all road-rail vehicles of the type that caused the Tebay accident are now fitted with an automatic braking system, and any without this safety system are banned from our tracks. We have also been working closely with the RMT union on engineering from scratch a secondary protection system for our track workers."

Chapter 34

2007 GRAYRIGG: POTTERS BAR CRASH 'REPEATED' IN CUMBRIA

There were striking similarities between the Potters Bar disaster in 2002, as described in Chapter 31, and the derailment of a Virgin Pendolino in Cumbria five years later, again resulting in loss of life.

On February 23, 2007, the 5.30pm Virgin West Coast Pendolino service from Euston to Glasgow, consisting of Class 390 unit No. 390033 *City of Glasgow* and nine coaches carrying 105 passengers and four staff, was travelling at 95mph through Cumbria when it was derailed by a faulty set of points at Grayrigg, immediately after crossing Docker Viaduct at 8.15pm. The carriages began rocking and swaying violently before the tilting train left the rails and careered down an embankment near Little Docker Cottage, with the first coaches jack-knifing. Seconds later Margaret Masson, 84, lay dying, her daughter Margaret Langley beside her, crying out, "Mum! Mum! Mum!" She passed away in hospital shortly afterwards. A total of 58 people were injured, 30 seriously. A family liaison centre was set up at Glasgow Central for worried relatives.

The train's derailment caused severe damage to the West Coast Main Line's overhead line equipment and tripped the entire circuit between Brock, near Preston, and Tebay, bringing several other services to a halt with all signalling equipment immediately turning to danger in accordance with the system's fail-safe design. First ScotRail's Caledonian Sleeper was curtailed and passengers transferred to overnight coaches. Within three hours of the derailment, the crash site of the accident was sealed off with a five-mile cordon. Up to 500 rescuers attended the scene, along with at least 12 ambulances, five fire engines, three RAF Sea King search and rescue helicopters, the International Rescue Corps, three civilian mountain rescue teams plus RAF Leeming Mountain Rescue Team and one Merseyside Police helicopter. Thermal imaging equipment was used to scan the train to ensure that there was no one still inside, and it was reported as being evacuated around midnight. However, the rescue operation was hindered by rain and darkness; access problems were caused by the narrow country lanes and muddy fields, while the emergency vehicles experienced difficult conditions, some needing to be towed by farm vehicles or tractors after becoming bogged down in mud. The recovery operation was slowed by problems with getting heavy lifting gear to the site, which required temporary roads to be constructed.

Dawn showed that while the entire train had been derailed, the rear carriages were standing nearly vertically on the sleepers and ballast. Standard class and the front five carriages were worst affected, with the rear four first-class carriages in better condition. The driving motor coach was lying on its side at the foot of the embankment. The central part of the train had toppled sideways down the embankment.

Virgin Group chairman Sir Richard Branson visited the site at 11am and said that he regarded driver Iain Black from Dumbarton as a hero, as he had tried to stop the train and stayed in his seat to ensure the safety of passengers. The driver had been trapped for about an hour while specialist cutting equipment was used to free him from his cab and he remained in hospital until late March. Branson added: "If the train had been old stock then the number of injuries and the mortalities would have been horrendous." The carriages were moved from the site between March 1-4. The line closure that followed the initial service suspension saw most Virgin services terminate at Preston or Lancaster from the south, with buses to Carlisle and all stations along the route. The only exception was an early-morning and late-evening through service from Carlisle to London and return, diesel-hauled via Blackburn and the Settle and Carlisle line. The Caledonian Sleeper was diverted via the East Coast Main Line, along with freight services. West Coast Main Line services began running on the line again on March 12 subject to a 50mph speed restriction at the crash site.

THE POINTS WERE NOT INSPECTED

Although the accident killed far fewer people than some other accidents on the West Coast Main Line, it had a major negative impact on Network Rail's safety record. Following the derailment, the Office of the Rail Regulator served an Improvement Notice on Network Rail's track inspection regime. The initial conclusion reached by the Rail Accident Investigation Branch was that the derailment was caused by a faulty set of points, 2B on the Down main line, controlled from Lambrigg ground frame 660 yards south-west of the accident site and used only occasionally. The stretcher bars, which hold the moving blades of the points the correct distance apart, had been found to be disconnected or missing. One was not in position, another had nuts and bolts missing, and two were fractured, leading to the loss of gauge separation of the point switch blades. Worst of all, a scheduled inspection on February 18 had not taken place and the faults in the points had gone undetected, Network Rail admitted, amid claims that inspection staff were overworked and under-resourced. The report recommended Network Rail to research any links between "long working hours and the propensity for human error during safety-critical tasks".

Experts compared the cause to that of the Potters Bar crash in 2002. Network Rail chief executive, John Armitt, said that the organisation was, "devastated to conclude that the condition of the set of points at Grayrigg caused this terrible accident" and apologised, "to all the people affected by the failure of the infrastructure." As a result, Network Rail checked more than 700 sets of similar points across the entire network as a "precautionary measure", saying later that "nothing of concern" had been found. The RAIB report noted that the Network Rail New Measurement Train ran over the site on February 21. This train uses lasers and other instruments to measure track geometry, overhead line height and track gauge. While it is not used to inspect points, it takes a video record of the track, which can be reviewed later. It was suggested that the video might have shown the defect but Network Rail said it would take most of a month to watch one day's worth of data. However, Labour MP John McDonnell said: "The fact that Network Rail apparently had footage of a missing stretcher bar days before the fatal crash is very worrying." Bob Crow of the National Union of Rail, Maritime and Transport Workers said: "We argued this train should not replace visual inspections. Inspectors who walk the track are the eyes and ears of the railway. They don't just check the safety of the track, they look at the area surrounding it, checking for signs of potential trouble such as gaps in the fence where vandals could get in."

NETWORK RAIL FINED £4 MILLION

In connection with its own investigation, the British Transport Police arrested and bailed three Network Rail employees, one in July 2007 and two in November 2007. However, on February 9, 2009, the British Transport Police announced that none of the three were to be charged following advice from the Crown Prosecution Service. On January 13, 2012, the Office of Rail Regulation announced that Network Rail would be prosecuted under the Health and Safety at Work Act 1974 for, "the company's failure to provide and implement suitable and sufficient standards, procedures, guidance, training, tools and resources for the inspection and maintenance of fixed stretcher bar points." At Lancaster magistrates' court on February 29, 2012, Network Rail indicated an intention to plead guilty to the charges, and at Preston Crown Court on April 4 that year, it was fined a total of £4,118,037 including costs. Passing sentence, Mrs Justice Swift said: "This was a very serious offence and could have easily led to greater loss of life than actually occurred." She added: "The importance of implementing safe and adequate systems for the inspection and maintenance of the infrastructure is paramount, in order to ensure that accidents like the ones at Potters Bar and Grayrigg do not occur."

On the same day that Network Rail was prosecuted, John Armitt was accepting a knighthood awarded in the 2012 New Year Honours list for services to engineering and construction, a coincidence that did not go unnoticed in the media. Network Rail chief executive Sir David Higgins said: "The Grayrigg derailment in 2007 resulting in the tragic death of Mrs Masson was a terrible event. Within hours it was clear that the infrastructure was at fault and we accepted responsibility, so it is right that we have been fined. Nothing we can say or do will lessen the pain felt by Mrs Masson's family but we will make the railways safer and strive to prevent such an accident ever happening again. Since the accident, much has changed in the way we plan and carry out maintenance work with new systems put in place to improve the quality and safety of our railway."

Ian Prosser, Director of Railway Safety at the Office of Rail Regulation, said the Grayrigg disaster, "was a devastating and preventable incident which has had long-term consequences for all involved." He added: "Under Sir David Higgins' leadership, Network Rail is focused on driving safety measures and I welcome the company's progress on implementing safety recommendations made after this incident. But the pace of carrying out improvements has, at times, been too slow and the rail regulator has had to repeatedly push the company to bring about change. Britain's railways are safe; one of the safest in Europe. But there is absolutely no room for complacency. Where failings are found those at fault will be held to account, and the entire rail industry must continue to strive for improvements to ensure that public safety is never put at a similar risk again."

In the aftermath of the tragedy, Network Rail carried out a major review of the quality of its maintenance procedures and implemented new systems. However, in 2014, Westmorland and Lonsdale MP Tim Farron called for a public inquiry into the Grayrigg train derailment, saying he feared that lessons had not been learned and that a review carried out after the crash seven years earlier was a "missed opportunity" to look at the safety of points on lines nationwide. The points that caused the derailment, and points 2A on the opposite line, were removed from the track following the derailment, and the line is now welded continuously for 2.2 miles. In 2013 the British Transport Police posthumously awarded a Chief Constable's Commendation to its North-Western Area media and marketing manager Jon Ratcliffe for his handling of media inquiries in the aftermath of the crash. He had died in 2008 following a sudden illness.

A RECONCILIATION TAKES PLACE
On October 29, 2012, the BBC's *Inside Out* documentary series reported that not only had Margaret Masson's son George forgiven the Network Rail maintenance manager from Preston who had forgotten to check those points, but the pair had become friends. Dave Lewis admitted at a hearing that he was "under pressure" before the crash, with

his team under-staffed and workers not given the right tools or enough time to carry out checks. He said he had sent an email to his bosses a year before the crash, in which he described the inspection system as a "shambles". The jurors heard how an inquiry ruled the "immediate cause" of the crash as being that the train had gone over a "degraded and unsafe" set of points, known as Lambrigg 2B. Mr Masson, who attended the inquest, had gone with hatred in his heart towards Mr Lewis, but that changed when he heard the evidence. "I stood up and the coroner asked if I had anything to say and I told him: 'For what that man tried to do I respect him – I'll have a drink with him any time,'" he told the BBC, which later took Mr Lewis to Glasgow to meet the Masson family.

INDEX